Our First Family's Home

T0164408

Our First Family's Home

The Ohio Governor's Residence and Heritage Garden

EDITED BY MARY ALICE MAIROSE

PHOTOGRAPHS BY IAN ADAMS

BOTANICAL ART BY DIANNE MCELWAIN

FOREWORD BY GOVERNOR TED STRICKLAND
AND FIRST LADY FRANCES STRICKLAND

AFTERWORD BY HOPE TAFT, FIRST LADY EMERITA

*With contributions by Guy Denny, Dewey Hollister,
Gary W. Meisner, and Barbara Powers*

Ohio University Press

Athens

in association with

The Friends of the Ohio Governor's Residence and Heritage Garden

Ohio University Press, Athens, Ohio 45701

www.ohio.edu/oupress

© 2008 by Ohio University Press

Botanical art © 2008 by Dianne McElwain

Original photographs © 2008 by Ian Adams

Historic photographs courtesy of the Ohio Historical Society

OHIO
HISTORY

OHIO HISTORICAL SOCIETY

Printed in Ohio

All rights reserved

Ohio University Press books are printed on acid-free paper ⊗ ™

15 14 13 12 11 10 09 08   5 4 3 2 1

Frontispiece: Residence from the Bog Garden

Library of Congress Cataloging-in-Publication Data

Our first family's home : the Ohio Governor's Residence and Heritage Garden / edited
by Mary Alice Mairose ; photographs by Ian Adams ; botanical art by Dianne McElwain ;
foreword by Governor Ted Strickland and First Lady Frances Strickland ; with contributions
by Guy Denny ... [et al.].

　　p. cm.

　Includes bibliographical references.

　ISBN-13: 978-0-8214-1790-4 (hc : alk. paper)

　ISBN-10: 0-8214-1790-8 (hc : alk. paper)

　ISBN-13: 978-0-8214-1791-1 (pa : alk. paper)

　ISBN-10: 0-8214-1791-6 (pa : alk. paper)

　1. Ohio Governor's Residence (Columbus, Ohio) 2. Ohio Heritage Garden (Columbus,
Ohio) 3. Ohio Governor's Residence (Columbus, Ohio)—Pictorial works. 4. Ohio
Heritage Garden (Columbus, Ohio)—Pictorial works. 5. Columbus (Ohio)—Buildings,
structures, etc. 6. Architecture, Domestic—Ohio—Columbus. 7. Governors—Ohio—
Biography. 8. Historic gardens—Ohio—Columbus. 9. Landscape gardening—Ohio—
Columbus. 10. Endemic plants—Ohio. I. Mairose, Mary Alice. II. Adams, Ian, 1946–
III. McElwain, Dianne.

　F499.C78O45 2008

　977.1'57—dc22

2007038902

Contents

Foreword

Governor Ted Strickland and
First Lady Frances Strickland

THE history of the current Ohio Governor's Residence and Heritage Garden is both educational and entertaining in its account of our first family's home's almost human struggle to endure. Homes and gardens are dependent on humans, and in the case of a governor's residence and garden, the family that lives there changes every eight years or less. As you will learn, each family brings its own distinct tastes and contributions to the integrity of the property.

A historic restoration specialist recently suggested that the Ohio Governor's Residence has three stories to tell: the story of the structure itself along with the furnishings and memorabilia of the family that gave it to the state; the history of Ohio artists and artisans whose work is displayed; and the history of the house as a home for the governors and their families. A fourth story was added during the Taft administration when First Lady Hope Taft made a concerted effort to reflect all of Ohio's diverse landscapes through the creation of the Ohio Heritage Garden. These four stories combine to make the Ohio Governor's Residence and Heritage Garden a living museum.

Garden entrance at sunrise

This book tells these four stories in a way that shows the evolving nature of the home and garden. It begins with the embarrassing situation in 1917 that led to the legislature's decision to provide a permanent home for Ohio's governors and chronicles the move from the original home on Broad Street to the current property on 358 North Parkview Avenue. The stories of the architectural design and style of the house, the evolving interior changes through nine different administrations, and the transformation of the grounds into a heritage garden are told by those who best know them.

The metaphor of the Governor's Residence's struggle to survive is seen in the need for each administration to respect the Residence as a public facility and protect it accordingly, while at the same time living there gracefully. The state tends to the basic maintenance of the house and grounds. Those things that make a home comfortable and a public facility inviting, however, have generally been provided by the residents with the help of generous individuals and private entities whose donations of time, expertise, and resources greatly improve and enhance the property.

The first families' personal stories are fun to read. They come not only from the governors and first ladies but also from the children, who gave us the memorable stories of an alligator in the bathtub and a tree house created as a special birthday gift. Also interesting is the way each family changed the interior of the house to accommodate its particular needs and taste. The styles of decorating were influenced by factors ranging from faithfulness to the period of the house, to what was in vogue at the time of a particular administration, to sturdiness for meeting the demands of a young family.

The most difficult period for the Residence was the eight years it was unoccupied and fell into significant disrepair. Fortunately, the "bones" of the house were robust enough to withstand the neglect. The Celeste administration recognized both the historic significance and current potential of the house and went to great lengths to restore it to its original elegance. Through a variety of resourceful means, First Lady Janet Voinovich brought unique pieces to the Residence: some items were gifts from the last private owner, others were acquired from state agencies, and many were remarkable tag sale finds.

The story of the Heritage Garden reflects not only the essence of Ohio's geological and physiographic systems, but also forward-thinking commitment to sustainability and alternative sources of energy. We are continuing this commitment by incorporating "green" strategies in all plans for future structural improvements to the fullest extent allowed and possible.

After the efforts of four successive administrations to improve the Residence and Heritage Garden for the people of Ohio, the first families' home is coming into its own. Public tours are available and welcome, and specially trained docents share the Residence's stories with visitors.

On behalf of all the families who have called the Residence home, we are happy to welcome you to visit the Residence and Heritage Garden through this book. We hope that you enjoy this trip through history and that you will join us in our efforts to make this public treasure the best it can be.

Virginia creeper leaves

Acknowledgments

MANY people and organizations have contributed to the success of this book. The families of both the private owners and the governors who have called the Residence home have generously shared their memories and recollections to give us a greater appreciation of the history of the Residence. We would like to thank the Friends of the Ohio Governor's Residence and Heritage Garden for their leadership and support of the book. A grant from the Louise Taft Semple Foundation has allowed the Friends to make this publication a reality.

Several friends have carefully read some or all of these essays at various stages in the editorial process. Betsy Burke, Joyce Hathaway, Barbara Meister, Lee Ann Parsons, Tod Ralstin, Phil Sager, Rick Stanforth, and Leslie Stephany have all improved the book with their astute suggestions. Kay Jeffrey, Stephen Jeffrey, The Ohio Historical Society, the Ohio Department of Development, the *Columbus Dispatch,* and the Robert E. and Jean R. Mahn Center for Archives and Special Collections at Ohio University have all provided historic photos for use in the book. Finally, we wish to thank the staff at Ohio University Press for their encouragement and expertise.

Facing page: Asters in the Prairie Garden

Right: Lilacs in bloom

Page xii: Flowers bloom on the trunk of a redbud tree

Our First Family's Home

one

The Architecture of the Ohio Governor's Residence

Barbara Powers

> Those soft, beautiful houses which affect us by their perfect repose and harmony . . . their feeling of rest and simplicity—no stress or striving here, only peace and quiet. Nowhere are there such houses as these.
>
> —Allen Jackson, *The Half-Timber House*[1]

THE Ohio Governor's Residence, originally the home of industrialist Malcolm D. Jeffrey, reflects the lifestyle of businessmen and industrialists living in the suburban community of Bexley in the early twentieth century. Completed in 1925, the house was designed by Columbus architect Robert Gilmore Hanford in the Jacobethan Revival style. A stately residence surrounded by spacious landscaped grounds and gardens, the house reveals the architect's familiarity with historical design precedents and a concern for unity of design, quality of materials, and craftsmanship associated with country estate living during the early twentieth century.

From the end of the Civil War until well into the twentieth century, Ohio enjoyed a strong economy and tremendous population growth, reflecting the growth experienced by the United States as a whole. Location, natural resources, cheap energy, plentiful labor, and unrivaled transportation routes that included Lake Erie, the Ohio

Front door decorated for fall

3

River, the canal system, and railroads made Ohio a leader in America's industrial growth. At the beginning of the twentieth century, Ohio's political, industrial, and economic influences reached throughout the country, making it one of the most powerful and diverse economic centers in the United States. By 1930, Ohio was the fourth-most-populous state.[2] The prosperity and industrial power Ohio experienced from the mid-nineteenth century until the onset of the Depression had brought urban growth and suburban expansion: as urban centers became more crowded and congested and the means of transportation improved, development of the affordable land just beyond the edge of the city introduced planned residential neighborhoods and the large impressive homes of industrialists.

Early prototypes for the layout of suburbs were mid-nineteenth-century rural cemeteries such as Spring Grove in Cincinnati, Lakeview Cemetery in Cleveland, and Green Lawn Cemetery in Columbus. The cemeteries' picturesque landscape designs, curving paths, and planned vistas are echoed in the design of early suburban developments such as Glendale, Ohio, near Cincinnati.

Mid-nineteenth-century picturesque romantic ideals were expounded by Andrew Jackson Downing, among others, in *The Architecture of the Country House,* his pattern book presenting Italianate and Gothic Revival designs and introducing what would become the American ideal—a single-family detached house situated on a landscaped lot in a rural setting.

This suburban development continued into the early twentieth century. Bexley's development illustrates these broad patterns of suburbanization in its pastoral setting along Alum Creek just east of Columbus, its accessibility to major transportation routes, and its pattern of subdivision into landscaped residential lots. Even its name, from a parish in the county of Kent, England, evoked a rural picturesque image.

The early 1900s brought the interurban electric railway and trolley car service from downtown Columbus out to Bexley as well as the growing use of automobiles, providing transportation for businessmen from their downtown offices to the doorsteps of their Bexley residences. Bexley was established as a village in 1908. Parkview, Columbia, Drexel, and College were the first streets laid out. The community exemplified early twentieth-century suburban planning principles

Fall colors reflected in a window

Back lawn

and community amenities in its enforcement of building codes and in its paved streets and street lighting. By 1921 the population of Bexley had grown to two thousand, and in 1931 it became a city.[3]

As neighborhood growth and suburban development created a high demand for housing, early twentieth-century residential architecture reacted against what was seen as the excesses and extremes of Victorian-era taste. Architects relied instead on an eclectic borrowing of historical design features drawn from European and American Colonial models alike, but emphasizing the accuracy and unified presentation of the stylistic details, high-quality materials, and craftsmanship. House designs imitating those of European nobility and our own early American founders were adapted to affluent and middle-class suburban homes and likewise became popular expressions for affordable small house designs in the 1920s and 1930s. In part the popularity of these historically influenced houses came from examples of the work of both English

Carriage house
with solar array

and American architects published in professional architectural journals but also widely disseminated through the popular culture in architectural plan books and magazines such as *Ladies' Home Journal, House Beautiful,* and *House and Garden.* Many soldiers returning from World War I had seen firsthand the romantic, picturesque villages and manor houses of England and France. No matter what the architectural source of the design, these Period Revival–style houses conveyed a strong message of symbolism, lineage, and history as well as taste and pedigree—all important factors conveying individual character and economic achievement that could not be better expressed than visually through one's own "castle."

The Ohio Governor's Residence reflects these early twentieth-century architectural trends as an example of the Jacobethan Revival style. This stylistic label, combining Elizabethan and Jacobean, was coined by architectural historians to describe early twentieth-century architecture borrowing details and features from late medieval English examples and the domestic architecture generally associated with the sixteenth- and

Kitchen shelves
looking into
dining room

The house under
construction
(circa 1923–25)
*Photo courtesy of
Stephen Jeffrey*

seventeenth-century reigns of Elizabeth I and James I. This style is also referred to as Tudor, Half-Timber, Elizabethan, Jacobean, and Old English.[4] The influence of these historic English-derived design sources is immediately apparent on arrival at the Ohio Governor's Residence. The exterior walls are a combination of stucco and native limestone with smooth Bedford stone for the quoins defining the corners, capping the projecting gables, and surrounding the windows and entrance. Decorative half-timbering on portions of the upper floors coordinates the architectural details of the original garage staff living quarters with the main house. The steeply pitched slate gable roof is pierced with several large molded brick chimneys.

The two-story gable front entrance projection extends toward the curved driveway. The oak front door is carved in small panels and surrounded by a stone Tudor arch with engaged columns and carved rosettes. Inside the front door, the unity of design between the exterior and interior is apparent. As in a baronial manor, the entrance hall features a slate stone floor, oak beamed ceiling, carved oak paneling, and a staircase with carved balustrade of open strapwork patterns, on the landing of which one can pause at the bay window to look through the leaded glass panes to the garden. Flanking the entrance hall are the dining room and the

Redbud tree at
the front door

The dining room under construction (circa 1923–25)
Photo courtesy of Stephen Jeffrey

slightly sunken living room, each displaying oak paneling, decorative plaster ceiling details, carved stone fireplace mantels, and bay windows with leaded glass and oak surrounds. These spaces are meant to be reminiscent of the medieval great halls.

It was not uncommon for such Jacobethan houses to have what could be thought of as two main elevations—the streetside front entrance elevation, which is the more public façade; and the garden elevation, typically to the rear and side of the house. The unity of design is further expressed between the outside and inside through the garden elevation and the garden "rooms." These extensions of the interior plan that formed the original portions of the garden landscape included an open terrace along the back of the house that stepped into garden beds defined by low stone walls. Later the terrace was enclosed to create a large room and a smaller screened-in porch.

Architect Robert G. Hanford published *A Selection of Photographs Illustrating Part of the Work of R. G. Hanford, Architect,* highlighting a hotel, apartment building, and several Bexley houses, including the Malcolm D. Jeffrey House. As an introduction to a series of advertisements for Columbus- and Ohio-based materials, craftsmen, and equipment used in his projects, he states, "Materials, like men, are judged by

The rear patio before the space was enclosed (circa 1925–35)
Photo courtesy of Kay Jeffrey

Dining room—
Taft adminis-
tration

their associates. Just as an Architect is judged by the buildings he designs—the Builder by the building he constructs—the Craftsman and the Artisan by their workmanship —so are materials and equipment judged by the buildings of which they are a part."[5] In the Ohio Governor's Residence the architect's choice of quality materials included stone, oak, stucco, slate, decorative plaster details, built-in bookcases and window seats, and ornamental iron light fixtures designed in a period fashion.

It is important to note that while such houses built in the first half of the twentieth century conveyed the outward appearance of a time past, they were designed as modern homes with up-to-date spaces and features including central heating, kitchens, multiple bathrooms, and structures of wood or steel framing, reinforced concrete, or, in the case of the Residence, hollow tile construction.

The Ohio Governor's Residence reflects in its architecture and garden landscape the rich history of Ohio. Recognized in the National Register of Historic Places, the Residence is worthy of preservation because of its significant architectural design, craftsmanship, and history associated with a central Ohio industrialist family and their descendants. The Residence has many stories to tell of early twentieth-century suburbanization and residential development in Bexley and of the governors and their families who have called the Residence home.

Notes

1. Allen Jackson, *The Half-Timber House* (New York: McBride, Nast, 1912), quoted in Mark Alan Hewitt, *The Architect and the American Country House* (New Haven: Yale University Press, 1990), 78.

2. Additional information about these themes in Ohio history can be found in George W. Knepper, *Ohio and Its People* (Kent, OH: Kent State University Press, 1989), and Eugene H. Roseboom and Francis P. Weisenburger, *A History of Ohio,* 2nd ed. (Columbus: Ohio Historical Society, 1996).

3. Edith Mae Hamilton Herrel and Lavada Kuhn Hogg, *Bexley Images* (Bexley, OH: Bexley Historical Society, 1978).

4. Several sources for additional information about American architectural styles are Rachel Carley, *The Visual Dictionary of American Domestic Architecture* (New York: Henry Holt, 1986); Alan Gowans, *The Comfortable House: North American Suburban Architecture, 1890–1930* (Cambridge, MA: MIT Press, 1986); and Virginia and Lee McAlester, *A Field Guide to American Houses* (New York: Alfred A. Knopf, 1984).

5. *A Selection of Photographs Illustrating Part of the Work of R. G. Hanford, Architect* (Columbus, OH: Denny A. Clark, n.d.).

Foyer—Strickland administration

two

The History of the Residence

Mary Alice Mairose

AN embarrassing situation led Ohio's General Assembly to secure a permanent executive residence. From 1803, when Ohio became a state, until 1920, governors were responsible for finding their own housing. Most stayed in hotels or rented houses while the General Assembly was in session. In December 1916, newly elected governor James M. Cox discovered that W. D. Fulton, the secretary of state–elect, had rented the house that Cox had planned to live in during his term in office. To avoid further such embarrassments, House Bill 559 was enacted on March 30, 1917. A board composed of past governors James E. Campbell, Myron T. Herrick, and Judson Harmon was authorized to purchase a suitable lot where the new governor's mansion could be built. Although a tract of land on East Broad Street was purchased, the original legislation was amended to allow the state to purchase an existing structure.

Two years after the original bill was signed, the state purchased the Georgian-style brick house at 1234 East Broad Street that had been built in 1905 for Charles H. Lindenberg. The child of German immigrants, Lindenberg made his fortune as one of the founders of M. C. Lilley and Company, which manufactured fraternal regalia.

Ohio buckeye in bloom

Noted Columbus architect Frank Packard designed the house. Alterations were made to the structure in the remaining months of that year. At the same time, inmates at the Ohio State Reformatory in Mansfield made furniture for the residence. In early 1920, Governor Cox moved into the Mansion with his family and became the first of ten governors to live there, followed by Harry L. Davis, A. Vic Donahey, Myers Y. Cooper, George White, Martin L. Davey, John W. Bricker, Frank Lausche, Thomas Herbert, and John W. Brown.

Garden room— Taft adminis- tration

The Lindenberg house comfortably served Ohio's first families until the mid-1950s. However, by then the area surrounding the mansion had become more commercial and the house needed major repairs that were not covered in the state budget. After the official residence of Ohio's governors was re-located to Bexley, the Ohio Historical Society used the Broad Street building for the State Archives for a dozen years. Later, it served as a restaurant and office space before it was purchased as a home for the Columbus Foundation in 1987 and carefully restored.

State seal in great room

A Generous Offer

The Bexley area was largely rural during the nineteenth century, but the area quickly developed into an exclusive residential community. Capital University moved to Bexley in 1876, and in 1898 sewer and water lines were put in for nearby Camp Bushnell, a camp used to muster in volunteers headed to Cuba during the Spanish American War. By 1921, the population of the village was 2,000, and this number more than tripled during the 1920s. One individual to take up residence in the 1920s was Malcolm Jeffrey, the youngest child of Joseph A. Jeffrey, founder of the Jeffrey Manufacturing Company, which made coal-mining equipment. Nicknamed "Captain Jack" in honor of the military rank he achieved during the First World War, Malcolm Jeffrey served as manager of the export division of his family's company. In 1923, Jeffrey commissioned Robert Gilmore Hanford to design a house in the Jacobethan Revival style. Hanford, a Columbus architect, designed several buildings in central Ohio, including other houses in Bexley and the Rocky Fork Hunt and Country Club in Columbus. Jeffrey, his wife, the former Florence Rodgers, and their two small sons moved into the new house on North Parkview Avenue in 1925. Sadly, Malcolm Jeffrey lived only five years in his new home. He died in 1930 at the age of forty-six. His widow and sons remained in the house for six more years.

In 1936, Florence Jeffrey Carlile, Malcolm Jeffrey's sister, and her husband, William Wilson Carlile, who served as chief counsel for the Jeffrey Manufacturing Company, purchased the home. They added a master suite on the second floor, enclosed the back patio to create both a large room overlooking the garden and a screened-in porch, and planted the first rose garden on the property. Following the death of Florence Jeffrey Carlile in 1954 (her husband had died in 1941), the house passed to the Very Reverend Charles U. Harris, husband of the Carliles' daughter Janet. The Harrises, who lived in Evanston, Illinois, where Harris was an Episcopal clergyman and dean of the Seabury-Western Theological Seminary, decided to offer the house to the state for use as an executive residence in 1955. Governor Frank Lausche accepted the offer on behalf of the state of Ohio, on condition that the house would be used as a governor's mansion for twenty-five years or ownership would revert to the Harrises.

C. William
O'Neill with his
wife, Betty, and
two children
*Courtesy of the
Ohio Historical
Society SC 3653*

A New Home for the Governor . . . and an Alligator: The O'Neill Administration, 1957–59

Elected in 1956, C. William O'Neill was the last Ohio governor to serve a two-year term and the first to occupy the new Governor's Mansion. His family, consisting of wife Betty and their two elementary school–aged children, did not move into the new mansion until March, after extensive redecorating. The main floor, which was open to visitors, featured a living room decorated with blue carpet and draperies. Foyer

Off the living room was a music room and a large back room furnished with wrought-iron furniture covered with cheerful fabrics. The dining room contained an oriental rug and furniture given to the state by Mrs. Carlile's heirs. The second floor contained the family's bedrooms, offices for the governor and first lady, a private living room, and a small kitchen.

Newspaper reporters were invited to tour the newly furnished home and declared that it suitable for the first family. After seeing the bathtub and the eleven-headed shower in the bathroom used by the O'Neills' son, a re-

16

Living room

porter for the *Ohio State Journal* declared that C. William Jr. would be the "cleanest kid in town if he does not drown." Memorable visitors included Cincinnati television personality Ruth Lyons of *The Fifty-Fifty Club*, who broadcast an episode of her show from the Mansion, and Dave Garroway, who taped an episode of *The Today Show* dealing with education. Since people from around the state wanted to see the new mansion, First Lady Betty O'Neill hosted countless groups who came to the Mansion for luncheons and teas.

With two young children in residence, the Governor's Mansion was a lively place during the O'Neill administration. Betty O'Neill recalled that the children had a wide assortment of pets during their father's term as governor: dogs, cats, rabbits, and canaries all shared the house with the family. Even an alligator, a gift from Congressman Chalmers Wylie, lived in one of the bathtubs for a short time. The children also had hamsters, which sometimes escaped from their cages and surprised guests at important meetings. Mrs. O'Neill recounted that after having been asked several times how her children liked living in the Mansion, she put the question to her young son, who replied, "Well, it's a roof over our heads."[1]

Family and Famous Folks:
The DiSalle Administration, 1959–63

Michael DiSalle of Toledo, elected in 1958, noted that his wife, Myrtle, was not eager to move into the Mansion, which he described as being a "pile of mongrel architecture" and "hardly a cozy nest." In spite of these shortcomings, the house offered plenty of space for the DiSalles' five adult children and their rapidly growing families. Mrs. DiSalle converted both the offices used by Governor and Mrs. O'Neill and the second-floor sitting room into guest bedrooms.

Michael DiSalle was the oldest child of Italian immigrants. His six younger siblings and their families were frequent guests for family dinners in the spacious back room of the Mansion. Their brother's election may have seemed the embodiment of the American dream. Family members marveled that the boy who could not speak English when he started school was now governor of Ohio. The DiSalles started a

Governor DiSalle and his wife, Myrtle, with children and grandchildren, Christmas 1959
Courtesy of the Ohio Historical Society
P-90

John F. Kennedy;
Ted Kennedy;
William Cole-
man, Ohio
Democratic State
Chairman;
Maurice Connell,
assistant to Gov-
ernor DiSalle;
John M. Bailey,
Connecticut
Democratic State
Chair; and Gov-
ernor DiSalle in
the governor's
study, 1959
*Courtesy of the Ohio
Historical Society
P-90*

tradition at the Mansion by holding wedding receptions for two of their daughters in the backyard.

The staff at the Residence consisted of inmates from the Ohio Penitentiary, most of whom were serving life sentences for murder. Initially, the DiSalles were uncomfortable with this arrangement, but in time they formed strong friendships with the men. DiSalle recalled his wife conducting daily inspections of the work of the houseman, lawn man, and chauffeurs that "would have done credit to the most hardboiled top sergeant." She also taught the men, who had no previous kitchen experience, how to cook such delicacies as *poulet Marengo* and *paella valenciana*. The men became great favorites of the DiSalle grandchildren and have been remembered by family members as gentle, affectionate baby sitters. The men were not above sneaking treats of ice cream to the children between meals against Mrs. DiSalle's strict orders.[2]

Early in the campaign for the presidential election of 1961 some Ohio Democrats considered nominating DiSalle as the presidential candidate. John F. Kennedy recognized Ohio's importance in gaining the nomination and visited DiSalle at the Mansion in 1959 for a steak dinner and a discussion of the upcoming election. DiSalle met the party on the front steps and first greeted Jack Kennedy. He then turned to Kennedy's younger brother Ted and said, "Ed, I always keep hearing you are the bright member of the family."[3] The meeting did not go as Kennedy had hoped, because he failed to secure DiSalle's promise of Ohio's support. However, by the time of the Democratic Convention, DiSalle led the Ohio Democratic Party in support of Kennedy.

Due to DiSalle's national prominence, many other noted political leaders visited the Mansion, including Senator Hubert Humphrey of Minnesota. The Reverend Martin Luther King Jr. visited DiSalle in 1963. Boxer Rocky Marciano attended an event at the Mansion, delighting the staff. Advice columnist Ann Landers, a friend of the family, and her daughter were invited to attend the wedding of one of the DiSalle children. Unfortunately, Landers got the date wrong, and mother and daughter came the week before the wedding. Mrs. DiSalle invited them to dinner and to stay overnight. Landers's daughter recalled being a nervous wreck on discovering that the members of the house staff were inmates serving life sentences.[4]

Governor DiSalle and Martin Luther King Jr. on the Residence grounds
Courtesy of the Ohio Historical Society
P-90

Opening the People's House: The Rhodes Administration, 1963–71

DiSalle lost his bid for reelection in 1962, and the next governor was James A. Rhodes. Born in Jackson County, Rhodes had a long association with Columbus politics, having been elected mayor of Columbus while still in his thirties. He served as auditor of state for a decade before his election as governor.

Rhodes and his wife, Helen, moved into the Mansion with their three teenaged daughters. Extensive redecorating took place to bring the décor up to the current fashion. The original slate and wood floors in the foyer, living room, dining room, and music room were covered with avocado green carpets. Years later, Mrs. Rhodes informed her successor, Dagmar Celeste, that the carpets were put down to ease her back pain from hours spent standing on the slate floors in receiving lines.[5] Curtains and upholstery throughout

Foyer—Taft administration

Governor
Rhodes with his
wife, Helen, and
children and
grandchildren
*Courtesy of the Ohio
Historical Society*
P-95

these rooms featured shades of green, white, and beige, reflecting popular styles of the 1960s. The floor of the large room at the rear of the house was covered with rust carpeting, and rust floral draperies hung at the windows. The major change made during the Rhodes administration, however, was the 1969 conversion of the screened-in porch to a sun room by replacing the screens with large windows. This room was decorated with a celery green carpet and draperies, and the wrought-iron furniture was covered with bright floral fabric.[6]

During their years at the Mansion, the family entertained the people of Ohio and celebrities alike. Monday through Thursday, Mrs. Rhodes hosted teas for groups of 250 to 300 women each day. Folding chairs were brought into the garden room for these events. Large formal dinners were held in the back room or under tents in the backyard. Up to two thousand people were welcomed for summer garden parties. During the Ohio State Fair, many of the fair entertainers were dinner guests at the Mansion. Bob Hope, Pat Boone, Art Linkletter, and Lionel Hampton were among the notable visitors during this period.

The Rhodeses had their share of family events at the Mansion. Both of the Rhodeses' older daughters were married during their father's term in office, and their wedding receptions were held in the Mansion and Gardens. Mrs. Rhodes loved the holidays. Every year, the Rhodeses hosted an Easter Egg Hunt for members of the media and their families. At Christmas, Mrs. Rhodes decorated a large Christmas

Governor
Gilligan with his
wife, Mary
Kathryn, and
children
*Courtesy of the Ohio
Historical Society SC
2691*

tree in the living room with ornaments she made during the year. Like the DiSalle family before them, the Rhodeses formed close attachments to the Ohio Penitentiary inmates who staffed the Mansion. The men were treated as members of the family and even referred to Helen Rhodes as "FL," the nickname Governor Rhodes bestowed on his wife in honor of her position as first lady. Eleven trustees generally staffed the house and grounds, some of them living at the Mansion while the rest were transported each day from the prison.

Highlighting Ohio at Home: The Gilligan Administration, 1971–75

Following the eight years that the Rhodes family lived in the Mansion, John Gilligan and his family took up residence in 1971. Governor Gilligan and his wife, Mary Kathryn, known as Katie, were natives of Cincinnati. Their four children were young adults by the time their father became governor, and did not live at the Mansion. Mrs. Gilligan charted a new course for the state's first ladies, moving the position away from a social role to an activist role. During her four years as first lady, she was an advocate for reform of Ohio's mental health system, a role that brought her national recognition.

Because Governor Gilligan focused on refurbishing the Statehouse during his time in office, he and Mrs. Gilligan made no significant changes to the Mansion beyond basic maintenance. They ended the practice of having inmates live on the grounds and were the first to have full-time security on the property. Wishing to have significant pieces in the Mansion to highlight Ohio's history, the Gilligans made arrangements with the Ohio Historical Society to have the silver service from the U.S.S. *Ohio* on display at the Mansion. The Ohio Arts Council arranged for artists from around the state to have month-long exhibitions of their works at the house. Mrs. Gilligan was an accomplished cook, who frequently took a turn cooking in the Mansion's kitchen. She also supervised plantings on the house grounds, including a weeping cherry tree that still graces the front yard.

Governors' Grove
in fall

The Gilligans began to entertain members of the General Assembly and their wives in an effort to break the ice between the governor, a Democrat, and the Republican legislature. In 1973, George McGovern, the Democratic candidate for the presidency, was scheduled to speak to Democratic county chairmen at the Mansion. McGovern was delayed, and Gilligan attempted to keep his guests—most of whom would have preferred a different candidate—entertained. The candidate arrived about two hours late. While McGovern was speaking to the guests, Senator Hubert Humphrey of Minnesota—whom McGovern had defeated in the Democratic primary for the nomination—phoned to say he was in town and asked if he could spend the night. Gilligan extended the invitation, and as a result, the two political rivals ended up spending the night under the roof of the Ohio Governor's Mansion!

Carrying on the tradition, started by the DiSalles and continued by the Rhodeses, of celebrating family weddings at the Mansion, the Gilligans' older son and older daughter were married there. Their daughter Kathleen, who married Gary Sebelius on New Year's Eve of 1974, became a political figure in her own right and was elected governor of Kansas in 2002. Governor Gilligan and Governor Sebelius are the first father and daughter in the United States to both hold this position.

An Empty House:
The Rhodes Administration, 1975–83

In 1974 James A. Rhodes was elected to a third term as governor. Four years earlier, the Rhodeses had purchased a new home in Upper Arlington, a western suburb of Columbus. Comfortably established in their new quarters, the Rhodes family decided not to move back into the Mansion. In an article from January 9, 1975, the *Columbus Dispatch* cited myriad leaks and the difficulty of heating the Mansion as reasons that Rhodes and his family chose not to reoccupy the house.

Between 1975 and 1983 the Mansion was used for official entertainment and rented out to various groups for events ranging from business meetings to fashion shows. Very little was done to maintain the house during this period. A former convict who had been pardoned by Governor Rhodes served as a live-in caretaker but lacked the necessary resources to maintain or improve the property. Since the state still owned the old Governor's Mansion on Broad Street, many questioned the wisdom of Ohio's maintaining two executive residences, especially since both houses stood empty and the state was in a period of financial difficulty.

A March 15, 1979, article in the *Dispatch* announced that Governor Rhodes wished to sell the costly Governor's Mansion to the city of Bexley. Rhodes suggested

Governor Celeste
with his wife,
Dagmar, and
children on the
front steps of
the Residence
*Courtesy of the Ohio
Historical Society
State Archives
AV4161*

that Bexley could use the property for a senior citizens center or that the state could sell the house and its surrounding acreage. There was some discussion about giving future governors a housing allowance instead of furnishing an executive mansion, but this proposal was never carried out.

New Life for an Old House: The Celeste Administration, 1983–91

The Celestes were the first to use the name Governor's Residence, abandoning the more pretentious term "mansion." The *Akron Beacon Journal* of November 5, 1982, reported that in spite of stained carpets, buckled linoleum, soiled upholstery, and several nonworking appliances, Mrs. Celeste was excited

by the prospect of her new home. "It's better than what I live in now," she told a reporter. As a mother of six children, she especially relished the fact that each bedroom had its own attached bath, which would eliminate typical morning arguments over which child got first chance at the shower.

Upon moving in, the family was overwhelmed by the condition of the house: the showers did not work; wiring in some parts of the house had melted and the rest could not bear the load of the rooms; much of the plumbing was no longer functional; very little usable furniture was left; and the mattresses that remained were badly mildewed. Worse, silverfish infested the bathrooms, and cockroaches and rodents had taken up residence in the kitchen. Unable to sleep on her first night at the Residence, Mrs. Celeste went to the kitchen for a cup of tea. When she turned on the light, the floor came to life: cockroaches scuttled into the woodwork, but a small rat remained, stunned by the bright light.[7] On another occasion a bat was discovered in the private living quarters, and the governor was forced to dispatch it with a tennis racket. Before a luncheon meeting, the newly hired residence manager found water coming from the dining room chandelier. With Governor Celeste's help she managed to get the water and electricity shut off, and then set up a table in another part of the house.

Governor's study
with furniture
designed
by Stephen
Bucchieri
*Photograph by Steve
Harrison, Depart-
ment of Development*

In March 1983 the Celeste administration established the Friends of the Residence, a nonprofit organization to restore and enhance the property. The friends included representatives from such organizations as the Ohioana Library, the Ohio
Arts Council, the Architects Society of Ohio, the Ohio Historical Society, and the
Bexley Historical Society. Although fundraising was the group's primary purpose, it
also worked to recognize the significance of the Residence and to ensure that Ohio
arts, crafts, and literature were represented in the house.

For the first time in the history of the Residence, the staff was not composed
primarily of inmates. Ten dedicated staff members worked to repair and refurbish the
house. While the state paid for painting and wiring, many necessary repairs were not
covered by the state budget. Generous donations to the Friends of the Residence
from individuals and companies around the state made possible a complete overhaul
of the house. Major projects included removing the existing carpeting; stripping,

Governor's
study—Taft
administration

refinishing, and sealing the wood floors; and sandblasting and sealing the slate floors in the foyer, great room, and garden room. The Friends also paid to replace the wood flooring in the dining room, which had become warped by years of leaks. Oriental rugs donated for use in the Statehouse during the Gilligan administration were laid over the refinished floors. The kitchen also required major renovations, as most of the appliances no longer worked and the old metal cabinets barely hung on the wall. An Amish craftsman installed capacious wooden cabinets, and professional-quality appliances were put in, transforming the kitchen into an inviting and efficient room.

Since much of the furniture was lost or destroyed during the eight years that the house stood empty, the Celestes had to start almost from scratch to decorate the house. The Friends of the Residence commissioned Cleveland-area architect Stephen Bucchieri to design pieces for the public rooms. Observing that executive residences in other states were furnished with expensive antiques that seldom had any connection to the state's history, Dagmar Celeste wanted strong, sturdy pieces

Kitchen

that would withstand heavy daily use. Moreover, she wanted pieces designed by an Ohioan especially for the Residence and made by Ohio craftspeople. Bucchieri used the proportions of the grids of the windows and wood paneling as a historic reference in designing the simple contemporary pieces. In her book *We Can Do Together,* Dagmar Celeste describes the pieces as having been influenced by the work of Scottish architect Charles Mackintosh, a leader of the Art Nouveau movement. Some of these pieces are still used by the state in the offices of the Department of Administrative Services.

To further highlight the talents of Ohio artists, the Celestes worked with the Ohio Arts Council to arrange a yearly exhibit of works by artists from around the state. Ohio pieces acquired for the Residence's permanent collection include a quilt by textile artist Nancy Crow, a native of Loudonville. An intricate design of contrasting colors, patterns, and textures in broken lines and broken circles makes the quilt's title, *Contradictions,* especially appropriate. Mrs. Celeste experienced some trepidation when central Ohio artist

Detail of *Contradictions* by Nancy Crow

Alfred Tibor offered her a sculpture for the Residence in honor of her work with peace education. Tibor, a native of Hungary who lost most of his family in the Holocaust, was known for serious works focusing on the suffering of Holocaust victims, and Mrs. Celeste did not know how the public would react to such a subject in the garden of the Governor's Residence. However, she was delighted with the artist's new work,

and the statue *To Life* still stands in the garden today. Dedicated to the "memory of the children who died in the Holocaust so that all children will remember," the piece depicts a family consisting of a mother, father, and three children. The statue is surrounded by crabapple trees, and when their flowers bloom in the spring, the inscription at the base of the work becomes especially evocative. Taken from the Book of Genesis, the passage reads, "I will make your descendants as many as the stars of Heaven."

Living room

Crabapples in
bloom

The Three Sisters
by Joan Wobst

The grounds and gardens were bleak and barren after years of neglect: the grass was brown and the old rose garden was overgrown. Improvements to the grounds included planting six redbud trees around the house, one in honor of each of the Celeste children. Raised vegetable beds were installed at the rear of the property, and an herb garden with brick walls was built by artist John Spofforth of Athens, Ohio. The president of the Rosarian Association approached Dagmar Celeste and offered his assistance with the Rose Garden. He carefully dug up each plant and washed its roots before replanting it in fresh soil and taught Mrs. Celeste how to care for the roses.

Beyond making physical alterations, Dick and Dagmar Celeste were the first to recognize the cultural potential of the house. They saw behind its flaws a place of beauty and significance, a place to bring people together, a place of which the people of Ohio could be proud. Recognizing the importance of the property, the Celestes had the house listed on the National Register of Historic Places. Although previous first families had opened the house for teas and luncheons, the Celestes instituted the practice of conducting tours of the Residence and garden on Tuesday afternoons, welcoming busloads of people from around the state. They also opened the house for readings with poets and authors as well as monthly chamber music concerts.

The Celestes also used the Residence for official entertaining. International visitors included European ambassadors, Asian representatives, and other world leaders. The Oni of Ife, spiritual leader of the Yoruba people of Nigeria, made Governor and Mrs. Celeste Yoruba chiefs in 1988. American dignitaries were also entertained at the Residence. During the presidential campaign of 1984, Celeste hosted a pig roast for Walter Mondale, the Democratic candidate. The event drew nearly one thousand people. Other significant guests included the Reverend Jesse Jackson and former first lady Rosalynn Carter. Among the notable writers to visit the Residence were May Sarton, Maya Angelou, and Nikki Giovanni. Several entertainers visited during the Celeste administration, including Peter, Paul, and Mary, Arlo Guthrie, Pete Seeger, and Ohioan Kaye Ballard. Comedienne Lily Tomlin was an especially memorable dinner guest. Initially feigning awe at being a guest of the governor, Tomlin surprised everyone at the table by hanging a spoon on her nose. When Governor Celeste asked her to show him how to do the trick, she obliged; but unbeknownst to him, she passed the spoon over a candle flame each time she presented him the dropped spoon. After multiple attempts, the governor's face was covered with soot, sending the other guests into gales of laughter.

During the Celestes' eight years at the Residence, most of their six children lived in the house at least part of the time. The Celestes celebrated their youngest child Stephen's seventh birthday with an elaborate party and the gift of a tree house in the backyard. For years, the tree house served as the setting of many sleepovers for Stephen and his friends. Major family events held at the Residence included the wedding of the Celestes' son Christopher in the garden in 1987 and a wedding reception for his brother Eric the following year.

Governor and Mrs. Celeste with Walter Mondale
Courtesy of the Ohio Historical Society State Archives AV 4161

Tree house given to the Celestes' youngest child as a birthday present
Courtesy of the Ohio Historical Society State Archives AV 4161

George and Janet
Voinovich listen
to a speaker
during an event
at the Residence
Courtesy of the Mahn
Center for Special
Collections, Ohio
University

A Foundation for the Future:
The Voinovich Administration, 1991–99

The next occupants were George and Janet Voinovich of Cleveland. Before his election as governor, Voinovich had served as mayor of Cleveland. Since the Friends of the Residence was terminated at the end of the Celeste administration, the Voinoviches established a nonprofit organization, called the Governor's Residence Foundation, to raise funds for enhancements to the property. Janet Voinovich turned her attention to refurnishing the Residence in keeping with the period in which it was built and the Jacobethan Revival style of the house's original design. Guided by advice from William Seale, the former White House curator, who was serving as a consultant on the restoration of the Statehouse in the 1990s, and with the aid of staff from the Ohio Historical Society, the Voinoviches based many of their design decisions on photographs taken of the interior while the house was a private residence. They followed the intent of 1920s Revival homes, namely to suggest a well-maintained English manor house that utilized furniture and ornaments belonging to several generations.[8] Under Seale's direction, the "Buckeye Suite" was commissioned. Consisting of a settee, chairs, and stools, the pieces were made in the Jacobean tradition with representations of buckeye branches as part of the decoration.

With a sharp eye for bargains, the first lady haunted tag sales and antique shops searching for appropriate furniture. Pieces formerly used in the superintendent's house

at the old Massillon Psychiatric Institution found a new home at the Residence, along
with furniture made by inmates at the Mansfield Reformatory in the early twentieth
century. Janet Harris, daughter of William Wilson and Florence Jeffrey Carlile, the last
private owners of the property, generously donated several pieces she had inherited
from her mother's estate. The Voinoviches acquired several pieces of art pottery made
in Ohio by the McCoy, Rookwood, and Roseville potteries for display in the governor's study. Mrs. Voinovich discovered a painting by Morgan County native Howard
Chandler Christy in a warehouse at the Ohio Historical Society. Entitled *The Summit*,
the large canvas portrays Christy's lover Elise Ford and the couple's daughter Holly.
The Governor's Residence Foundation paid to have the painting restored, and it is now
on permanent loan to the Residence.

When the house required a new roof, the state contributed the cost of regular asphalt shingles and the Foundation raised additional funds to obtain the slate roof, which
was historically and architecturally more appropriate. In
order to assure the long-term preservation of the house, the
Voinoviches started the Governor's Residence Advisory
Commission. Composed of historians, architects and staff
from the Ohio Department of Administrative Services, the
Commission is charged with preserving the Jacobethan Revival
character of the property. Any changes made to the property must be approved by the Governor's Residence Advisory Commission.[9]

The Summit
by Howard
Chandler Christy
hangs over the
staircase

Voinovich Bell

An avid gardener, Governor Voinovich called for the garden to be enlarged. The governor enjoyed working in the vegetable garden, tending tomatoes, lettuce, and zucchini. He invited children from a local elementary school to help plant and tend potatoes. At the end of the growing season, the children were rewarded with bags of potatoes to share with their families. A portion of the garden produce was given to a charity that provided fresh vegetables to needy families. The Voinoviches also planted several fruit trees and reseeded the lawn using an improved hybrid turf. Finally, the Voinoviches envisioned a greenhouse to allow the horticulturalist to nurture sickly plants and grow tender seedlings. The structure was built during the next administration, that of Governor Taft. Inmates from the Pickaway Correctional Institute began working in the garden as part of an apprenticeship program to gain certification in agriculture, a program that still thrives at the Residence.

The Voinoviches enjoyed their share of memorable events at the Residence. First Lady Barbara Bush visited Mrs. Voinovich for tea while in Columbus and also visited with the first lady's staff. The crew members of the space shuttle *Discovery* (STS-70), which went into space in July 1995, were also overnight guests at the Residence. Known as the "All-Ohio Crew," four of the five members were native Ohioans, and Governor Voinovich made the fifth, a native of New York, an "honorary Ohio Citizen." The next morning, they helped Governor Voinovich open the State Fair. Memorable family occasions included birthday celebrations for the governor's mother each June. The Voinoviches' eldest son was married at St. Joseph's Cathedral in downtown Columbus, and the reception was held at the Residence. Later, Governor and Mrs. Voinovich enjoyed spending time with their first grandchild in the spacious backyard of the Residence.

A Short Stay: The Hollister Administration, December 31, 1998–January 11, 1999

George Voinovich was unable to complete his full second term as governor because he became a U.S. senator on December 31, 1998. Nancy Hollister, lieutenant governor in the Voinovich administration, served the remaining eleven days of his term. She and her family, including her husband, Jeff, five children, and small granddaughter, moved into the Residence for this short period primarily to allow security and communications to stay at the Residence. The Hollister family had a New Year's Eve celebration and delighted in an unexpected snowfall.

Bob and Hope
Taft with daugh-
ter Anna in the
Appalachian
Garden
*Photograph by Chris
Kasson, Department
of Development*

Planting the Seeds: The Taft Administration, 1999–2007

Bob and Hope Taft moved into the Residence in 1999. Although Mrs. Taft initially described the Residence as a combination of museum, hotel, and assisted living facility, the Tafts eventually came to think of the Residence as home. They delighted in visits from their college-aged daughter Anna and family members from around the country. Like their predecessors, the Tafts entertained their share of notable guests. In 2000, then Governor George W. Bush of Texas was a guest while campaigning for the White House. Ohio-born opera singers Sylvia McNair and Kathleen Battle visited, as did Columbus native Jack Nicklaus.

Continuing the efforts of her predecessors, Mrs. Taft set about improving the property. Because her brother was confined to a wheelchair, Mrs. Taft was especially sensitive to the needs of those with disabilities. She made sure that one of the first major projects undertaken during the Taft administration was to make the property compliant with the Americans with Disabilities Act. Ramps were built by the front door and inside the house to provide wheelchair access. In the original design of the

Governor Taft
with George
Bush in the
governor's study
Courtesy of the
Columbus
Dispatch

Garage and fall color

house, the living room doors had opened into the back garden, but this openness was lost when the back porch was added in the 1930s. To recapture this earlier feature, French doors were constructed in place of the bay window in the great room, once again opening the rear of the house to a raised stone patio and the garden beyond. Students from a preservation program stripped and refinished the walls of the dining room to restore their original appearance.

Hope Taft's keen interest in Ohio's environment led her to make significant changes to the grounds. She worked with landscape designers and plant experts to develop the Heritage Garden, a series of small gardens which represent the diverse regions of the state. In 2006 the Heritage Garden was awarded affiliate status with the Lady Bird Johnson Wildflower Center. Mrs. Taft also wished to call attention to the emergence of the green industry in Ohio. Green Energy Ohio installed an all-Ohio solar array on the roof of the carriage house, which provides backup power for the Residence security system. Surplus energy generated by the array is sold back to the power grid.

To display the state's artistic heritage, Mrs. Taft instituted a loan program with museums around the state. Changing exhibits allowed visitors to the Residence to view works by Ohio artists Frank Duveneck, George Bellows, Robert Scott Duncanson, Clarence Holbrook Carter, and Henry Church, among others. Other acquisitions showcased Ohio industries, including lamps made in the late 1800s by the Fostoria

Glass Company and the donation of more pieces of Rookwood pottery. The Foundation also purchased a Baldwin piano made in Cincinnati for the Residence's permanent collection to replace the pianos previously loaned to the Residence by local music stores.

Mrs. Taft had special needlepoint seats designed for the Buckeye stools. Each of the four stools has a different design incorporating architectural features of the house and Ohio state symbols. For instance, Mrs. Taft made the seat cover that shows the state seal, a depiction of the sun rising over Mt. Logan in Ross County, and the design of the decorative ceiling in the living room. To bring the spirit of the Heritage Garden inside the house, Mrs. Taft and some friends created needlepoint seat cushions depicting various species of birds and flowers native to Ohio.

Soon after moving into the Residence, Mrs. Taft became interested in the history of the property. She began collecting photographs of the house from the time it was a private home and through the previous administrations. She also interviewed representatives of each family that had lived in the house. This increased interest in the history of the house emphasized the need for a staff member to document the ongoing history of the Residence. A grant allowed the Governor's Residence Foundation to engage a curator to catalog the furniture used in the house and to conduct further research on the history of the property. The curator developed a nonpartisan volunteer program for the Residence. Previous governors have had volunteers help

Ted and Frances
Strickland in the
backyard
*Photograph by Chris
Kasson, Department
of Development*

with events at the house, but the new program is designed to function independently of officeholder or political party. Docents attend a class about the Residence and Heritage Garden and must pass a test before they begin giving tours.

Like the Voinoviches, the Tafts continued the practice of relying on a private foundation to help with the upkeep and enhancement of the property, but because of Mrs. Taft's interest in developing the garden it became clear that a second fundraising organization would be helpful. The new organization is called the Friends of the Ohio Governor's Residence and Heritage Garden, a name that hearkened back to the Celeste years. Unlike the Governor's Residence Foundation, whose members are appointed by the governor, the Friends group is a nonpartisan membership-based organization that will provide continuity and support for the property.

New Directions: The Strickland Administration, 2007–

On moving into the Residence in January 2007, Ted and Frances Strickland, in recognition of the historic significance of the property, decided against having a partisan fundraising organization and strengthened the Friends of the Governor's Residence and Heritage Garden to serve as the sole support group for the property. Wishing to accord the house and the garden equal importance, they formed Residence and garden advisory committees. Frances Strickland supported Hope Taft's vision for the garden and invited her to chair the garden committee to see her efforts come to fruition.

Like the Voinoviches, the Stricklands were struck by the beauty of the Residence's English-inspired Jacobethan Revival architecture. They painted the foyer to emphasize the limestone doorways and the graceful curves of the ceilings in the front and rear entryways. Mrs. Strickland, an avid backpacker, selected the shamrock green color for the foyer, which, with the dark wood of the exposed beams, reminded her of the peacefulness of old-growth forests. Governor Strickland, having worked as a prison psychologist before entering politics, enjoys pointing out the exquisite craftsmanship of the pieces made by inmates at the old Mansfield Reformatory around the beginning of the twentieth century that Mrs. Voinovich brought to the Residence in the 1990s. Frances Strickland's love of music is reflected in the living room, where her guitar has found a home next to the Baldwin baby grand piano. Live music is now a part of all Residence events. Pianists volunteer their time to play at dinners and receptions, while larger events boast bands whose styles range from Celtic to country to jazz.

The Stricklands enjoy opening the Residence for both formal and informal entertaining and hosting events as diverse as cabinet meetings and author readings. They strive to make the Residence homelike and inviting, while maintaining the historic nature and the distinct Ohio flavor of the property. Like many of their predecessors, they work closely with the Ohio Arts Council to display works by historic and contemporary Ohio artists.

Mrs. Strickland's guitar with books from the Ohioana Library and a painting of Columbus artist Elijah Pierce

Upon moving into the Residence, the Stricklands were especially pleased with the solar panels on the carriage house roof and are constantly searching for other ways to make the house more energy efficient and environmentally friendly. Fluorescent lightbulbs, which use less energy than standard bulbs, are now used at the Residence. All disposable cups and utensils are made from renewable resources and are compostable. Rainwater is collected to water the plants, and a porous driveway will allow the underlying soil to absorb rainwater to nourish surrounding trees and plants and reduce the amount of water that goes into the storm drain. A planned extension to the existing carriage house will provide space for exhibits and other educational material, work and volunteer areas, and a gift shop. Among the environmentally friendly technologies that may be employed in the building are a green roof, partly covered with vegetation, and geothermal power, which is cleaner than energy produced by traditional fossil fuels.

THE GOVERNOR'S RESIDENCE has been home to nine first families, each of which has added its own layer of history to the property. Through their efforts, the property has developed into a place that is a showcase for Ohio, highlighting the state's history, art, industry, and environmental resources. Thousands of visitors tour the house and grounds each year, and leaders from around the country and around the world are entertained here by the first family. The Ohio Governor's Residence and Heritage Garden

Bluebells

is a representation of the state to these visitors: a place where schoolchildren learn about the natural diversity of their state and where visiting dignitaries can glimpse the proud heritage of the Buckeye State.

Notes

Much of the information in this chapter is drawn from interviews conducted with former occupants and staff members by Hope Taft in 2000 and by the author in 2006. Transcripts of these interviews are available in the Residence archives.

1. Betty O'Neill speech, Bexley Historical Society's Reminiscing Party, July 1975. Transcription by Bette Wallach, June 1986. A copy of the transcript is available in the Residence archives.

2. Michael V. DiSalle and Lawrence G. Blochman, *The Power of Life or Death* (New York: Random House, 1965 second printing), 135–41.

3. Howard Thompson, "Kennedy's Ohio Plans Uncertain," *Ohio State Journal*, September 16, 1959.

4. Margo Howard, *Eppie: The Story of Ann Landers* (New York: G. P. Putnam's Sons, 1982), 130.

5. Dagmar Braun Celeste, *We Can Do Together: Impressions of a Recovering Feminist First Lady* (Kent: Kent State University Press, 2002), 129.

6. Marilyn Hood, ed., *The First Ladies of Ohio and the Executive Mansions* (Columbus: The Ohio Historical Society, 1970), 28–29.

7. Celeste, *We Can Do Together,* 133.

8. William Seale to Mrs. George V. Voinovich, March 28, 1991. George V. Voinovich Collection, Ohio University Archives and Special Collections.

9. The Governor's Residence Advisory Commission was authorized by Ohio Revised Code 107.40, and went into effect September 29, 1995.

three

The Ohio Governor's Residence Heritage Garden Master Plan

Gary W. Meisner

THE Ohio Heritage Garden is a special garden for all Ohioans. Our rich ecological and geologic history provides the natural context and foundation for the Heritage Garden Master Plan. It is also inspired by the rich cultural history of the state and by its first families, who have dedicated their lives to unselfish public service.

The Garden vision recalls the forces of nature: mountains of ice that carved the land; lakes long past; ancient rivers whose courses have changed the region; the ebb and flow of plant communities, forests, prairies, and wildlife north and south through time; and today's unique storybook of ecological places and cultivated land that capture our imagination.

Virgin's bower blooms in the orchard

The Ohio Governor's Re

Landscape

MARYLAN

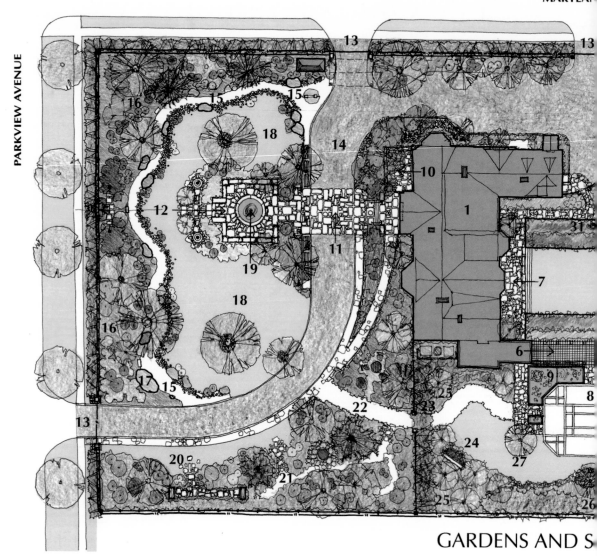

PARKVIEW AVENUE

GARDENS AND S

MEISNER
+
ASSOCIATES
L A N D
V I S I O N

GARY W. MEISNER, FASLA
LANDSCAPE ARCHITECT
DEWEY HOLLISTER
HORTICULTURIST
GUY DENNY
ECOLOGIST

1. The Residence
2. Carriage House
3. Gift Shop & Services
4. Greenhouse
5. Walled Garden
6. The Pergola

7. East Terrace
8. First Family Patio
9. Watergarden
10. West Terrace
11. Arrival Plaza
12. First Lady's Courtyard

13. Entry Gates
14. Visitor Queuing
15. Geologic Walk
16. Allegheny Garden
17. Glacial Erratic
18. Governors' Grove

19. Heritage Fountain
20. Meadow Garden
21. Woodland Wildflower
22. County Walk
23. Taxus "Wall"
24. State Seal

358 NORTH P
COLUMBU
JU

ENUE

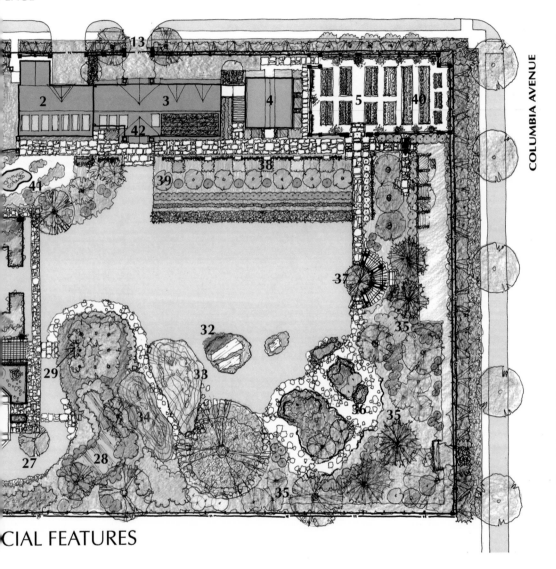

COLUMBIA AVENUE

CIAL FEATURES

25. Dogwood Glade
26. Tidal Basin Cherry Tree
27. Sister State Cherry Trees
28. Black Swamp Garden
29. "To Life" Sculpture
30. Prairie Garden

31. Jeffrey-Carlile Rose Garden
32. Alvar Rock Garden & Fen
33. Oak Openings Sand Dune
34. Headlands Sand Dune
35. Appalachian Garden
36. Edge of Appalachia Boulder

37. Johnny Appleseed Memorial
38. Earth's Harvest Agricultural Garden
39. Orchard, Berries & Bioswale
40. Cut Flowers, Vegetables & Containers
41. Kettle Lake Bog & Lost Plants Garden
42. Sun's Harvest Solar Arrays & Greenroof

KVIEW AVENUE
OHIO 43209
007

This Master Plan evolved from an idea initially driven by native plants to one that honors the following simple themes:

Left: Rose garden

Right: Birch tree

- Ohio's rich geologic and ecological roots
- Ohio's extraordinary culture of the land through agriculture
- Ohio's first families and their contributions in Ohio, across the nation, and throughout the world
- Ohio's connections with ecological history through our many preserves, arboretums, botanical gardens, zoological gardens, and heritage gardens
- The Jeffrey and Carlile families, donors of the residence and grounds
- Most importantly, the education of young and old about Ohio's great heritage

When the Governor's Residence moved from an earlier mansion on Broad Street in 1957, the "new" Residence inherited minimally landscaped grounds containing primarily ornamental plants mixed with a few native trees. There was no organized plan for the original landscape. A massive willow oak patiently symbolized our connection to the native past in the rear yard; oaks and a few native understory plants recalled some history in the front and side yards. The rear garden included a small rose collection reminding us of the Jeffrey family, who built the house, and the Carliles, who donated it to the people of Ohio. The grounds also included the carriage house, a small working garden in the northeast, and modest perimeter and foundation plantings. Added through time were several works of art, some temporary furnishings, and

Garden gate with wisteria

a small fanciful brickery garden. Perimeter fencing, historic low garden walls in the rear garden space, service structures, a contemporary patio in the rear yard, and drop-off drives also existed. That basic framework sets the stage for the current renovations and the new theme of the garden, "A walk around Ohio."

The Master Plan sets forth this theme of a walk around Ohio in a fairly simplistic way, utilizing the existing site framework of walls, walks, perimeter plant beds, and utility structures. A loop walkway encircling the site has evolved from existing paths, plant bed edges, service portals, and accessways. In the process of this evolution the walkway has become a symbolic "back road" of Ohio, weaving a succession of diverse gardens into one. In the following brief descriptions of the gardens, numbers in parentheses refer to the map of the Residence and Heritage Garden.

Arrival Area, Allegheny Garden, and Geologic Walk.

Visitors arrive for events and tours of the house and gardens at the main entry gate on the north edge of the property on Maryland Avenue, the side yard. A paved drive and roadway loop are being developed to greet visitors. The arrival area leads into the Governors' Grove (18) and Allegheny Garden (16). The Allegheny Garden, located on the northern and western periphery of the Governors' Grove, features plants and flowers of the beautiful Alleghenies in northeastern Ohio. The Geologic Walk (15) will edge the Allegheny plantings and serve

Left: Glacial
erratic boulder

Right: Red maple
in the Governors'
Grove

as an interpretive walkway connecting the arrival area to the woodland shade garden as it crosses the front lawn. Unique rocks and bedrock set along the path tell some of the many stories of Ohio's geologic history: a glacial striated stone from the Lake Erie islands, coal, sandstone, limestone, and the Cincinnati Arch will all be featured. A monumental sixteen-ton glacial erratic boulder (17), carried from the Canadian Shield by the glaciers, punctuates the walk's end.

First Lady's Courtyard

Plans call for a small courtyard (12) immediately adjacent to the arrival space. Set on an axis with the Residence's front door, it will align with the original drive from Parkview, and be flanked by two flagpoles and symmetric landscape plantings.

Governors' Grove

Encompassing much of the Front Lawn, the Governors' Grove (18) serves as a "forecourt" green space to the Residence and a grand setting for plantings by Ohio's governors. Past governors' trees and shrubs include the O'Neill locust, Rhodes taxus, Gilligan weeping cherry and star magnolia, Celeste river birch, Voinovich red oak and tulip tree, Hollister blue spruce, and Taft black tupelo and paperbark maple. Each new governor will add a special native plant honoring his or her family's residency.

Part of the
County Walk

Celeste Family Trees

The Celeste Family Trees, just inside the western entrance and adjacent to
the West Terrace, are eastern redbuds planted to honor the Celeste family's
six children.

Meadow Garden

A small perennial border garden (20) greets visitors as they leave the Geologic
Walk. Ohio Master Gardeners planted this area with native plants from various
parts of the state.

Woodland Wildflower Garden—County Walk

The Woodland Wildflower Garden (21) edges the southern border of the grounds.
It emphasizes deep shade plants, highlighted with woodland wildflowers. The
garden contains thousands of rescued plants. Artifacts and stones from each of
Ohio's eighty-eight counties are featured along the walkway (22). A clipped yew
topiary arch serves as a portal to the Dogwood Glade.

The Great Seal in the Dogwood Glade

The Dogwood Glade (25), located south of the Residence, features native flowering dogwood trees and the Great Seal of the State of Ohio (24), constructed in brick and donated by the people of Licking County.

First Family Patio

The First Family Patio (8) is south of the Pergola and main garden space. It provides a delightful retreat for the first family. The patio is surrounded by a diverse collection of trees. A clone of a Tidal Basin Yoshino cherry tree (27), which was brought to Washington, D.C., by First Lady Nellie Taft (1909–13), was donated by the National Arboretum, and provides a unique focal point and Ohio connection.

Right: Native wisteria on the pergola

Sister State Cherry Tree

An Oriental cherry tree donated by Ohio's sister state, the Saitama Prefecture in Japan, will stand near the First Family Patio.

The Water Garden

The Water Garden (9) with its six pools surrounds the Patio just south of the Pergola. The pools are filled with a diverse collection of native Ohio aquatic plants. Two large urns punctuate the corners of the Water Garden and serve as water recirculating points.

The Pergola

The historic pergola (6) was a primary element of garden architecture at the site, dating to the time it was a private home. It has been fully restored and incorporates several species of native vines and native bamboo.

East Terrace and Prairie Garden

The East Terrace (7) is located just behind and to the east of the Residence. French doors open onto the terrace and unite the house and garden. The Prairie Garden (30) flanks the west end of the East Lawn north and south of the restored formal Green. It provides an unusual ornamental display of native plants from Ohio's remnant prairies.

Jeffrey-Carlile Rose Garden and Wall Garden

Facing page: Rose garden at the rear of the Residence

The Jeffrey-Carlile Rose Garden (31) honors the families who built the Residence and donated it to the State of Ohio. A rose garden originally maintained in this area prior to 1957 has been restored by Ohio's rosarians and features award-winning varieties and Ohio-created hybrids. Across the walk is the Wall Garden, which features native crossvine, passionflowers, and Carolina roses.

Kettle Lake Bog and *Herb Garden*   Crabapple trees

The Kettle Lake Bog (41) recreates one of Ohio's rarest ecological environments. It features bittersweet cranberries, pitcher plants, and other unique native plants. Culinary herbs are planted throughout the brickery area and are used in food prepared at the Residence.

East Lawn

The East Lawn is the grandest open space on the grounds, serving as the main location for outdoor special events and ceremonies held at the Residence. It also serves as a recreational area for the first family. It is fringed by the "islands" and fen of the Sand Dune Gardens. Plans call for this area to be bordered by a unique bioswale and rain garden. These garden structures will serve to collect and treat storm-water runoff from the rear yard naturally, using Ohio native plants. Excess runoff will flow into the garden cistern.

Left: Asters blooming in the Sand Dune Gardens

Below: Mountain laurel in the Appalachian Garden

Appalachian Garden

The Appalachian Garden (35) highlights southeastern Ohio's link to the grand ecology of the Appalachian Mountains. Imported soils, limestone, and shale are used to recreate the several microclimates of that region. The Appalachian Garden represents the Edge of Appalachia Preserve.

Sand Dune Gardens and Alvar Rock Garden

Right:
The Sand Dune
Gardens

The Sand Dune Gardens, located near the southwestern corner of the East Lawn, recreate the unique flora along the shores of Lake Erie (34) and in the Oak Openings (33). Four islands of glacial striated bedrock (32) have been transplanted into the adjacent lawn, symbolizing Ohio's Erie islands. A small fen is interwoven into the "islands."

Robin perched in
crabapple tree

Johnny Appleseed Memorial

The Johnny Appleseed Memorial (37) is situated on the eastern edge of the
grounds and commemorates one of Ohio's greatest pioneers and the delicious
fruit he shared with America. A rustic arbor, sitting area, and interpretive panel
will tell this story.

Earth's Harvest Agriculture Garden

The Agriculture Garden (38) is located in the northeast section of the grounds
and features the Vegetable and Cut Flowers Garden (40). The garden also includes a greenhouse (4), a hotbed, and cold-frame cultivation areas. The Orchard
and Berry Garden (39), the Heritage Plants Garden, and Ohio hybrids demon-
stration area are being developed. Plans call for a new sustainable agriculture and
service building (3) that will incorporate a gift shop, exhibits, and meeting/
educational space. Cisterns will gather the runoff from the roof and recycle it
back to the plantings. A green roof and solar panels will cover the south-facing
roof structure (42). The Orchard and Berry Garden will contain several varieties
of berries, fruits, and nut trees found in Ohio, including pioneer varieties. Interpretive panels will tell each of these stories to the public.

To Life by
Alfred Tibor
surrounded by
daffodils

Art/Sculpture

Art and sculpture spaces are located throughout the site. The Heritage Garden Master Plan calls for the preservation of appropriate permanent artwork and establishment of the location and potential themes for heritage artifacts, suitable historic artwork, and temporary exhibits on the grounds.

THE HERITAGE GARDEN Master Plan borrows from the past, highlights Ohio's natural history and agricultural legacy, and incorporates sustainable principles. The Plan also sets a framework for developing educational programs, hosting outdoor events, preserving history, and providing a grand setting for the Residence.

four

A Tour of the Ohio Heritage Garden

Dewey Hollister

FIRST Lady Hope Taft conceived the idea for the Ohio Heritage Garden during the spring of 2001 when she first became aware of native plants and their benefits. With the help of landscape architects, garden designers, plant specialists, and garden clubs from around the state, she made her vision a reality. The Heritage Garden now demonstrates the beauty of Ohio's diverse landscape and educates visitors about how they can use native plants in their own home gardens.

The Heritage Garden captures the essence of Ohio. It showcases the unique areas of the state, which range from the sand dunes of Lake Erie to the rugged terrain of the Appalachian region, as well as types of habitats common to all of Ohio, such as woodlands and meadows (see appendix 1). The garden also features the fruits of Ohio's horticulture industry, exemplified by the agriculture garden, the rose garden, and the Governors' Grove. This chapter will take you on a tour of each section of the garden and introduce some of the plants that are featured there.

Prickly pear flower

Cardinal flowers
in Appalachian
Garden

Entry Gates

Upon entering the gates, visitors are greeted by the sight of annual beds that surround the front entrance of the house. These beds include peonies that were hybridized in Ohio.

Governors' Grove

The Governors' Grove is a special area of the grounds, facing the front of the house, where trees were planted by governors over the years. Fortuitously, most of these species are native to Ohio, even though that had not been a major selection criterion until the founding of the Heritage Garden. Each of these trees has a story to tell. The weeping Higan cherry, an example of a nonnative tree, is one of the only specimens known to have been planted during the Gilligan administration (1971–75). Six redbuds were planted by the Celestes (1983–91), in honor of each of their children. A very large honey locust, probably the cultivar 'Moraine,' was planted by Governor and Mrs. O'Neill (1957–59). The 'Moraine' is also an example of the work of Ohio hybridizers. It was developed in Dayton, Ohio, and was the first thornless honey locust to be patented (1949). One of the most recent additions is a Kentucky coffee tree, which was given to the Ohio Governor's Residence and Heritage Garden by Governor and Mrs. Fletcher of Kentucky.

Facing page:
Pin oak tree

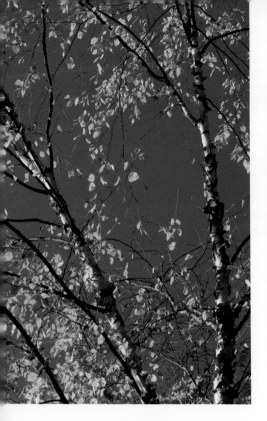

Detail of glacial
drop stone

Birch leaves

The Allegheny Garden

The Allegheny Garden, located on a strip of the front yard bordering the west and northwest fence line, represents the Glaciated Appalachian Plateaus of far northeastern Ohio. This area contains many species that live farther north in Canada or at higher altitude in places like the Allegheny Mountains of Pennsylvania. Plans call for a wandering path to serve as the centerpiece of the garden and tell the geologic story of Ohio. Already, a huge glacial drop stone (a six-ton boulder brought from Canada to central Ohio by the glacier) has been placed in the garden near the west gate and will serve as the other end of the path. This large piece of gneiss, a coarse-grained metamorphic rock, was dug up in a newly developing subdivision of Columbus and donated for use in the garden.

Although many existing trees and shrubs are not thematically correct, Allegheny plants are being added to this garden. The area around the rock features northern plants. Northern bayberry, while a common landscape plant, is native to only a few areas in northern Ohio. This largely Atlantic coastal shrub found its way into the state when Lake Ontario was an arm of the ocean. Striped maple, sometimes known as moose maple, is the poster species for the Allegheny Garden. The only place it is found in Ohio is in Ashtabula County in the far northeastern corner of the state. This maple is a very ornamental understory tree that is far more comfortable and common in Canada or the high eastern mountains. Its striped green bark marks it as one of

Common milk-
weed in the
Meadow Garden

the snakebark maples, which, except for this species, all occur in eastern Asia. As an example of a plant that has been in Ohio from the time of European settlement, this striped maple sapling grows in the area along with a hobblebush from the same part of the state. A running strawberry bush serves as a groundcover.

The Meadow Garden

The southwest corner of the grounds is now home to the Meadow Garden, designed as an English-style perennial border. Master gardeners from around the state have contributed plants native to their respective counties for this garden. Many of the beautiful plants in Ohio meadows are often considered weeds, and their common names reflect this attitude. Ironweed is a very tall plant with almost iridescent purple flowers that attract butterflies. Joe-pye weed looks like a group of tall pagodas, each topped with a ball of pink cotton candy. Common milkweed has beautiful spherical pink flower clusters and outstandingly architectural knobby pods. These flowers often attract monarch butterfly caterpillars, beautifully striped in yellow, black, and gray.

The Meadow Garden rivals any of the other gardens in length and beauty of bloom. Not bad for a bunch of "weeds"!

A central path, with benches at each end, is flanked by beds of meadow plants. This path connects to the trail network in the adjacent Woodland Wildflower Garden. The arrangement mimics meadows in the wild, which are usually next to woodland areas.

The Woodland Wildflower Garden

The Woodland Wildflower Garden was the first native plant area created in the Ohio Heritage Garden. In fact, it was one of the first gardens planted by Hope Taft, a lover of spring garden flowers, shortly after moving into the Residence. A large ginkgo, planted around the time the house was built, and the O'Neill honey locust provide shade for the area. The Wildflower Garden features rustic paths, mossy logs, and more kinds of woodland wildflowers than can be seen anywhere else in the state. Flowers have been donated by private landowners and others have been acquired by "plant rescue," operations in which plants are transplanted from an area threatened by development to a safer area.

Many of the wildflowers in this garden are spring ephemerals, so called because they die down to their roots by midsummer. The large-flowered trillium, Ohio's state wildflower and the Heritage Garden symbol, is a notable member of the early-to-rise,

Above: Dolls' eyes

Right: Trillium and violets

early-to-bed crew. Like all ephemerals, it races to capture a year's worth of light as soon as conditions are just warm enough for growth and before the light is blocked out by the trees' new leaves. Other wild-flowers keep their leaves for all or most of the growing season. Allegheny spurge, a favorite groundcover, is not only leafy during the spring and summer but often nearly evergreen. While this low, mottled plant looks nothing like the poisonous box-wood, deer can tell they are in the same family and will not eat it. Allegheny spurge is not considered native to Ohio, but since it occurs in adjacent states, it probably grew in Ohio at one time. The tall Canada violet blooms in the summer and some-times into the fall as well. Ferns thrive in the shade, and many species are represented in the Woodland Wildflower Garden.

The newest feature of this garden is the County Walk. All eighty-eight Ohio counties have contributed stone or brick artifacts to decorate this new link between the Woodland Wildflower Garden (front yard) and the Water Garden (backyard).

Dogwood Glade

A variety of the dogwood trees that grow in Ohio's forests are represented in the Dogwood Glade, including a tree with unusual yellow blossoms and berries, along with the more common pink- or white-flowered varieties. They surround a sculpture

Facing page:
Water Garden

Upper right: State
seal sculpture

of the state seal rendered in brick, which was presented to the Residence by the people of Licking County during the Voinovich administration. Irises hybridized by Ohioans grow in a bed across from the brick sculpture. Some of the flowers are named for notable Ohioans, including members of the first families who have lived in the Residence.

Lower right: Iris

Lower left:
Dogwood
flowers

The Water Garden

The Water Garden, which is still being developed, is located between the Family Terrace Patio and the Pergola. The patio is an island surrounded by three ponds, and the walkways are bridges connecting the patio to the rest of the grounds. These ponds will include Ohio's two water lilies, the fragrant water lily and the white water lily, as well as other plants representative of Ohio's native water species.

The Pergola

Mr. and Mrs. William W. Carlile, the last private owners of the property, added the pergola and flagstone floor in the late 1930s. For many years, exotic climbing vines covered the pergola, but they presented problems: Asian sweet autumn clematis invaded the rest of the grounds, while Asian wisterias steadfastly refused to bloom. Dagmar Celeste recalled that the wisteria did not bloom once during her eight years as

first lady. Native vines have now solved these problems on the pergola. The hummingbird-attracting trumpet creeper is displayed in three colors—'Minnesota Red', 'Flava' (yellow), and orange. All of the wisteria in the Heritage Garden is Kentucky wisteria, which generally grows near the Ohio River. In one growing season, many had reached the top of the structure, and they have bloomed profusely each year since being planted. From the same area, North America's only native bamboo enters Ohio from the south. Specimens of this plant were transplanted from the river town of New Richmond (Clermont County) and form a privacy screen along the entire south side of the pergola. The loss of once huge stands of giant cane (canebrakes) has been linked to the extinction of the passenger pigeon as well as the Carolina parakeet.

Trumpet creeper on the pergola

"To Life" Mound

At the east end of the pergola is a statue by Alfred Tibor, which was donated to the Residence during the Celeste administration, entitled "To Life." It is dedicated to the memory of the children who lost their lives in the Holocaust. Surrounding the statue are crabapple trees planted by Mrs. Celeste. Mrs. Taft planted daffodils, sometimes called the flower of hope. Some of these were hybridized in Ohio or named for notable Ohioans.

Sand Dune Garden

Male Hobomok skipper in Sand Dune Garden

The Sand Dune Gardens

The Sand Dune Gardens represent two very different habitats that lie in the Huron-Erie Lake Plains: the Lake Erie shoreline, represented by the Headlands Sand Dune; and the Oak Openings, a unique area west of Toledo, represented by the Oak Openings Sand Dune. The two gardens are separated by a sand path. The darker sands of the Headlands habitat range from neutral to alkaline and will feature Atlantic coastal plants such as American beach grass. Due to the exposed nature of these lake-edge areas, they are often high-energy environments. The Oak Openings is situated in an open forest, surrounded by trees that are fifty to sixty feet tall. Twelve thousand years ago, distinctive yellow-brown sand was deposited into a much deeper and larger Lake Erie. After the lake level dropped, this sand was blown into hills and ridges. The higher areas are dry and acidic, while the lower areas, or sedge meadows, are moist to wet. Notable plants in the Oak Openings garden include the gorgeous blue sundial lupine and prickly pear cactus. An old willow oak that dates to the period when the house was built provides shade for the sand garden.

The Alvar Rock Garden

Bare slabs of limestone or dolomite that
have been scraped clean by glaciers are the
habitats described by the term *alvar.* At first
glance, an alvar might resemble an abandoned air base with plants growing in random,
linear patterns. These alvar habitats, with their "lines" of plants, are of two main
types: cracks in the stone slabs and grooves scored into the pavement by rock-studded
glacial ice as much as a mile thick. As plants obtain a toehold, they slowly creep outward
over the flatter areas. Just to the east of the sand garden, the Alvar Rock Garden attempts to replicate this environment as an archipelago of raised stone islands. Several
massive slabs of limestone from the Marblehead Peninsula, together with some
smaller rocks, make up two islands. The larger one consists of slabs with glacial striations (smaller versions of glacial grooves) aligned in the original east/west configu-
ration. The smaller island is a slab containing numerous fossils that visiting children
love to examine.

  By far the most famous alvar plant growing in this garden is the Lakeside daisy.
Named for the town of Lakeside in northwest Ohio, this plant is found in only two
places on earth, the other one being in Ontario. For a federally endangered plant, the
gorgeous Lakeside daisy is exceedingly tough. The rare rock sandwort, another alvar
plant, looks like shaggy moss until it bursts into bloom; its flowers resemble miniature
baby's breath. At the base of the Alvar Rock Garden is a small fen composed of plants
that love the cold alkaline waters left by the glaciers.

Above left:
Lakeside daisy

Above right: Alvar
and Sand Dune

The Appalachian Garden

The Appalachian Garden is appropriately located in the southeast corner of the property. This garden represents unglaciated southeastern Ohio, sometimes known as the Appalachian Plateau. Two very different habitats are reflected in this garden. Acid soil plant communities are what many gardeners think of in connection with the Appalachian region. However, dolomite limestone (alkaline) outcrops, cliffs, and gorges represent very different plant communities, with some plants found nowhere else in Ohio.

The garden consists of several raised beds, created with appropriate stones, that provide an environment in which plants with very specific soil and drainage conditions can thrive. An area called the Blackhand Sandstone Outcrop consists of two beds: one is bordered by large sandstone blocks salvaged from a washed-out covered bridge near Zanesville; the other is retained by large chunks of Peebles dolomite from an abandoned quarry in Adams County. Plants featured in this area include such shrublike plants as the July-blooming great rhododendron, mountain laurel, and sourwood,

Sassafrass leaves

Willow oak

the reddest tree in the autumn mountains. Also of note are plants that University of Cincinnati botany and ecology professor Lucy Braun (1889–1971) collected from the Edge of Appalachia area in Adams County. The current owner of Dr. Braun's home donated several of these species to the Heritage Garden, including the rare hearts-bursting-open-with-love, wood hyacinth, and little brown jug.

In nature, the most spectacular elements of the dolomite cliff habitat are the house-size boulders that have fallen off the cliff face. These become aerial gardens, festooned with unique plants. A specimen that is now the jewel of this part of the garden came from a farm near Cincinnati. Wild orange columbines seem to drip off the boulder in the spring, and walking ferns stride across the mossy surface, cloning themselves wherever they step. The entire raised bed is called the Peebles Dolomite Outcrop. It is home to the evergreen shrub Canby's mountain-lover, so rare that only two genetic individuals survive in Ohio, remnants of the flora introduced into the state from the Carolinas by the ancient and now underground Teays River. Along with dolomite limestone and sandstone, pieces of coal and other rocks in this garden tell the geologic story of Appalachian Ohio.

The unraised areas contain plants that are easily grown, including both of the state's native buckeyes. Although the Ohio buckeye is the official state tree, the yellow buckeye is the variety preferred by gardeners because it keeps its leaves longer. Ohio's three indigenous magnolia species—bigleaf magnolia, umbrella magnolia, and cucumber magnolia—are also easily grown and featured in this part of the garden.

The Pioneer Garden

The focal point of the Pioneer Garden is a cutting-grown apple tree, taken from one of the last living trees planted by John Chapman, better known as Johnny Appleseed. Chapman, an early nurseryman, lived in central Ohio in the early 1800s and planted apple orchards across the state. Surrounding the tree are plants selected for their roles (good or bad) in the lives of the early settlers. Cotton has been grown at the Residence for several years. Besides giving people the chance to see the living plant, it helps illustrate the self-sufficiency demanded by life on the frontier. To produce clothing, one had to grow the cotton, pick out the seeds, spin it into yarn, weave it into cloth, then cut and sew it into a garment.

The Agriculture Garden

The Agriculture Garden occupies the northeast corner of the grounds, and celebrates Ohio's rich agricultural heritage. Originally planted by the Celestes, and enlarged by both the Voinoviches and the Tafts, the garden's many raised beds provide a healthy harvest of fresh vegetables for the kitchen and a place for cut flowers. Future plans call for this garden to be made much larger and feature rows of fruit trees, berries, and grapevines. This enhanced garden will focus on Ohio's farming past, present, and future.

A popular feature of the garden is Hammy Birthday Ohio, the bicentennial pig designed as part of the "Big Pig Gig," a community art festival held in Cincinnati in

Right: Bottle
gentian in the
Prairie Garden

2000. Sponsored by the Ohio Bicentennial Commission, Hammy's sides are decorated with paintings of a Bicentennial Barn and a cornfield to commemorate Ohio's agricultural history.

East of the Agriculture Garden is a greenhouse used to start new plants and nurse sick ones.

The Prairie Garden

Directly behind the Residence is the formal Prairie Garden. The Prairie Garden represents scattered areas in the western half of the state known as the Central Lowland Till Planes. These prairies are treeless, arid grasslands, and the plants that grow in these areas are quite hardy, having roots that grow ten to twelve feet deep. River run gravel was put down in the L-shaped beds to replicate this growing region, and beds plants are organized in mirror-image fashion.

Some continuous elements run the length of each bed to tie the design together. Little bluestem grass is planted in sinuous curves; in winter this grass is cut to half its height and all the other plants are cut down completely. The effect in snow is quite striking. In spring shooting stars and golden Alexanders usher in a new growing year. Ohio spiderwort and purple coneflower appear near the end of April. Early summer brings into bloom the compass plant; with leaves that align to catch the east and west sun and provide the prairie traveler with a handy way to establish direction. The New England aster brings the autumn show to an end sometime in November.

Facing page:
Prairie Garden in
the early fall

Contributions of Ohio botanists are also recognized in the Prairie Garden. Sullivant's milkweed, named for William Starling Sullivant (1803–73), the son of Lucas Sullivant, founder of Franklinton (now Columbus) and a noted botanist, blooms in the early summer. Lucy Braun's prairie dock blooms later in the summer. Riddell's goldenrod, which blooms from late summer to early fall, commemorates the work of John Leonard Riddell (1807–1965), who taught at the Cincinnati Medical College.

Rose Garden

"Betty Boop" roses

The Rose Garden

This garden is sometimes referred to as the Jeffrey-Carlile Rose Garden in honor of the families that built the house and donated it to the state. Mr. and Mrs. Carlile, the last private owners, planted the first roses on the property. Roses have grown in this garden ever since. During the Celeste administration, a rosarian tenderly dug up the roses planted by the Carliles decades before and cleaned their roots before planting them

in fresh soil. Sadly, soil-borne diseases killed these original roses and the garden was in need of revitalization. Once again, rosarians intervened with stunning results. One hundred twenty varieties of hybrid roses stand shoulder to shoulder in the Rose Garden today. They allow for comparisons among hybrid tea, floribunda, and grandiflora roses. The roses are grown pot in pot, a nursery growing system that has become popular with serious rose growers. Roses are planted in pots instead of the ground, allowing a high degree of control over soil and drainage. Each of these pots is sleeved inside another that always remains in the ground. This means the plants and their pots can be easily removed for maintenance, switched with other roses, or moved to a more sheltered storage area for the winter. Micro-irrigation probes in each pot allow exact control over the fertilizer and water.

Roses bred by Ohioans are also featured in this garden. Two Ohioans have had their roses selected as All-American Rose Selection (AARS) winners. 'Dream Come True,' bred by Dr. John Pottschmitt, one of the rosarians who had helped develop the garden, and 'Portrait,' bred by Carl Meyer, now grow in a special area near the main rose garden to display AARS-winning Ohio roses.

The Herb Garden and Kettle Lake Bog

The Herb Garden, built during the Celeste administration, provides a variety of culinary plants such as dill, parsley, sage, and chives. It is unlike the other gardens in being partially enclosed by walls. The stone wall connecting the house and the carriage house

predates the brick walls. An artist built new walls in the 1980s to create a partially enclosed space with a central fishpond. While not a formal "four-square" walled herb garden like those found in Europe, it creates that impression.

After the fishpond was equipped with a liner and partially filled with quartz gravel, it became a bog garden inspired by Cranberry Bog at Buckeye Lake. The bog was filled with acidic water and topped with peat, live sphagnum moss, and large cranberry. Since the water level in the bog must remain high, a standpipe was installed to allow for daily monitoring and easy filling. To this simple bog, many other unique plants were added, among them the exquisite bog orchid and the carnivorous northern pitcher plant, which is always a big hit with visiting children.

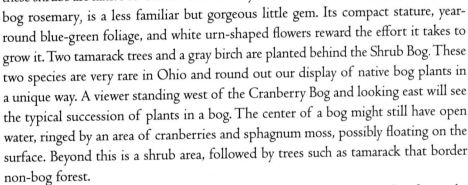

To maintain the bog theme, a shrub bog was installed in this area. Some of these bog species, including highbush blueberry, are well known to visitors, yet many do not realize that these shrubs are native to Ohio. The blueberry's distant cousin, bog rosemary, is a less familiar but gorgeous little gem. Its compact stature, year-round blue-green foliage, and white urn-shaped flowers reward the effort it takes to grow it. Two tamarack trees and a gray birch are planted behind the Shrub Bog. These two species are very rare in Ohio and round out our display of native bog plants in a unique way. A viewer standing west of the Cranberry Bog and looking east will see the typical succession of plants in a bog. The center of a bog might still have open water, ringed by an area of cranberries and sphagnum moss, possibly floating on the surface. Beyond this is a shrub area, followed by trees such as tamarack that border non-bog forest.

The Shrub Bog area is flanked by a raised planter of wild rice that forms the northeast border of the Herb Garden and Kettle Lake Bog. This planter is built to provide a canoer's-eye view of this giant annual grass so visitors can imagine what harvesting the seeds was like for Native Americans.

The Garden of the Lost

The Garden of the Lost illustrates the ebb and flow of plants, plant communities, and habitats over time. All of the plants in this garden were probably living in what is now Ohio more than two million years ago, before the Ice Age began. After one glacier or another receded, these species didn't make it back and so became lost to

Ohio. Some of the interesting plants in the Garden of the Lost include the familiar
sweetbay magnolia, a common landscape tree that enjoys wet conditions. Fur trappers
sometimes used its roots as bait in their beaver traps. Far less well known is the Florida
corkwood, North America's lightest wood, even lighter than cork. This tree is the only
one on the entire continent to have its own family, *Leitneriaceae,* and is the only species
in it. Not closely related to any other plant, it is believed to be descended from the
common ancestor of birch (*Betula*) and bayberry (*Myrica*). Discovered near Tuscaloosa
in 1958, Alabama snow-wreath looks like a low, feathery cloud in the spring. Its little
white pompom flowers continue sparingly throughout the growing season. For a rare
plant, this medium-size arching shrub is a vigorous grower and quickly makes a low
thicket from root sprouts.

The Wall Garden

Just north of the Ohio River, and following it in a narrow band, is the interior low
plateau, which has much in common botanically with the bluegrass areas of Kentucky.
Many of the plants growing there are common southern species that just manage a
toehold in Ohio. They like hot summers and relatively protected winters. The south

Crossvine

side of the east wing of the residence is a long, sunny masonry wall that creates a partial courtyard. West and northwest winds are blocked by the main part of the house, making this an ideal spot to grow some of these plants. Toward the east end of the wall garden is a southern magnolia, 'Bracken's Brown Beauty,' a species that may have been native to Ohio several million years ago. Crossvine is a perfect 365-day backdrop for anything else planted in the bed, due to its evergreen foliage and wall-climbing abilities. It sports beautiful red and yellow trumpet-shaped blooms, which appear in spring and orient themselves in one outfacing direction when the vine is grown on a wall. Some of the crossvine came from the Adams County property once owned by Nathaniel Massie, an early land speculator and politician. The crossvine is a backcloth to 'Ammon's Blue,' an Ohio cultivar of our native passionflower, which is found in southern Ohio and named for the author's daughter Ammon. Like all passionflowers, it is exotic in appearance. This particular cultivar is quite a bit larger in all its parts than the original species, and the flower is a deeper blue.

THESE GARDEN AREAS represent the diversity and beauty of Ohio's landscape as well as the history of the families who have lived at the Residence. As all the gardens continue to grow and mature, each season brings subtle changes. But the overall goal remains the same: to educate and encourage all citizens to save our natural heritage and to showcase our native plants in a residential setting.

five

Native Plants of Ohio

Dianne McElwain

A GOAL of the Heritage Garden is to educate visitors about the beauty and benefits of plants that are native to Ohio. The following pages present a selection of botanical art depicting some of Ohio's native plants that are featured in the Heritage Garden by award-winning botanical artist Dianne McElwain, of Cincinnati, Ohio, whose paintings are included in prestigious collections throughout the United States and abroad. Descriptions of the native plants represented here are included in appendix 2, "Native Plants of Ohio: Botanical Descriptions," by Dewey Hollister.

page 82
Native Plants of Ohio—The Prairie Heritage Garden, by Dianne McElwain.
From the Private Collection of David W. Haartz and Marilyn A. Fingerhut, Alexandria, Virginia. See page 119 for garden description

page 83
Native Plants of Ohio—The Meadow Heritage Garden, by Dianne McElwain.
From the Private Collection of David W. Haartz and Marilyn A. Fingerhut, Alexandria, Virginia. See page 120 for garden description

Native Plants of Ohio
The Prairie Heritage Garden

Dianne McElwain ©2006

Native Plants of Ohio
The Meadow Heritage Garden

Dianne McElwain ©2006

Bigleaf Magnolia

Magnolia macrophylla
Dianne McElwain ©2006

American Lotus   *Nelumbo lutea*   Dianne McElwain ©2004

Nelumbo lutea—American Lotus, by Dianne McElwain.

From the Private Collection of Kate Bolling and Jim Anderson, Portland, Oregon. See page 121 for plant description

pages 84–85

Magnolia macrophylla—Bigleaf Magnolia, by Dianne McElwain.

From the Collection of the Artist. See page 121 for plant description

Bignonia capreolata — Cross Vine, by Dianne McElwain.

From the Private Collection of Paul and Linda Groen, Bellevue, Kentucky. See page 123 for plant description

The Bog Heritage Garden
Dianne McElwain ©2006

Sarracenia purpurea
Pitcher Plant

Vaccinium macrocarpon
Cranberry

Sarracenia purpurea—Pitcher Plant and *Vaccinium macrocarpon*—Cranberry, by Dianne McElwain.

From a Private Collection. *See page 123 for plant descriptions*

Trillium grandiflorum—Large-Flowered Trillium, by Dianne McElwain.
From the Private Collection of Hope Taft, Dayton, Ohio. See page 125 for plant description

Passiflora incarnata — 'Ammon's Blue', by Dianne McElwain.

From the Private Collection of Ammon Hollister, Cincinnati, Ohio. See page 124 for plant description

Ohio Buckeye

Aesculus glabra

Dianne McElwain ©2006

Aesculus glabra—Ohio Buckeye, by Dianne McElwain.

From the Private Collection of David and Debra Hausrath, Fort Thomas, Kentucky. See page 125 for plant description

Erythronium americanum 'Trout Lily' Dianne McElwain #23©2005

Erythronium americanum—Yellow Trout Lily, by Dianne McElwain.

From the Private Collection of Roger A. Ward, Cincinnati, Ohio. See page 126 for plant description

Sanguinaria canadensis 'Bloodroot' Dianne McElwain #24©2005

Sanguinaria canadensis—Bloodroot, by Dianne McElwain.

From the Private Collection of Ed and Pat Sheppard, Sarasota, Florida. See page 127 for plant description

Afterword

LESSONS FROM THE OHIO GOVERNOR'S RESIDENCE AND HERITAGE GARDEN

Hope Taft, First Lady Emerita

If you plan for a year, sow rice.
If you plan for ten years, plant trees.
If you plan for a hundred years, educate the people.

—Chinese proverb

THIS proverb reflects the attitude of the caretakers of the house and grounds known as the Ohio Governor's Residence and Heritage Garden. Some changes have been made with only one administration in mind, while other improvements have been thoughtfully planned to last as long as the house stands. All have been added to help educate visitors about Ohio history in one way or another.

Each governor's term could be described as passing seasons in the life of the property. The early days of each administration are like springtime, when the house receives a good cleaning and a sprucing up so it feels like home to the new occupants. By the end of the term, autumnal sadness invades the grounds because the exiting family has learned to love the place despite any early qualms. Winter is at the doorstep when one governor leaves in January and the next one enters for the first time. Each

Bog Garden

Artist's fungus
on willow oak

new occupant adds history and works for the sustaina-bility of the facility, realizing that Ohio's governors serve not only as the head of state government but also as the steward of the house and garden they will call home dur-ing their time in office. It is an honor and a privilege, and it presents a wonderful opportunity to lead by example: to respect history and promote the future; to watch the changing seasons of the year as well as of political life; to distinguish what needs to be done for a day, a term, or eternity; and to make sure both the occupants and the facility age gracefully.

This is all brought into focus by watching the Heritage Garden throughout the year, as a lesson in sustainability and how nature plans for eons. All of nature works together to maintain a balance, ensure its future, and sustain life itself. Everything is in a perpetual state of being recycled and regenerated. Even the rocks that sustain liver-wort, lichen, moss, and emergent ferns are repeatedly buffeted by wind and rain and slowly eroding into sand. Plants need sand to ease their ability to take root. The Peebles Limestone Outcrop is an excellent place to see this cycle at work.

One realizes that nature has developed a way to nurture itself and its progeny if left to its own devices. The fallen leaves and decaying logs add nutrients to the soil that in turn provide food for new plants to grow. This can easily be seen in the Wood-land Wildflower Garden, where the leaves are intentionally left on the ground to decom-pose at their own pace and the logs quickly become covered with moss or mushrooms

Ice and leaf in
pool

and are attacked by insects. The large fallen tree trunk in the Appalachian Garden is one of my favorite places to see this process at work: a hollow section allows a look inside at the gradual process of decay; traces of insect paths are visible under the bark; and mold and fungus cling to its outer covering.

Winter plays its part in the cycle of sustainability. Its snows provide a warm blanket for tender roots and the deep moisture many need to germinate in the spring, while the cold stratifies seeds to make them ready to sprout when the ground temperature is just right. Without this season, many plants could not sustain themselves. The spicebushes in the Ap-palachian Garden and the native wisteria on the Pergola are examples of plants that need the hardness of winter to release their offspring. Not all is brown and bleak in the winter. The Cranberry Bog provides its best color and sustains the image of renewal when it's cold. The maroon pitcher plants are in

Prairie Garden
and Rose Garden

sharp contract to the lime green of the sphagnum moss and the red of the cranberry leaves. Add snow and this old fishpond becomes a living paisley.

Spring comes into its own when the ground temperature reaches 45 degrees. Some years we put a big thermometer in the East Lawn to see how much longer we have to wait. Seeing the Heritage Garden come back to life is a glorious experience. The early spring ephemerals, such as the Virginia bluebells and the trillium, in the Woodland Wildflower Garden race the catkins of the hazelnut in the backyard to herald its arrival. When the Lakeside daisies begin to bloom in the Alvar Rock Garden you know spring has arrived. The golden Alexanders and the shooting stars wake up the prairie. They try to outshine the soft pink of the Tidal Basin cherry near the First Family Terrace and the crossvine's yellow and red flowers on the Wall Garden. Not to be outdone, the Edge of Appalachia Boulder covers itself in a cloak of native columbine.

Summer brings a bright succession of color that lasts into the fall, especially in the Prairie Garden. Everything from the yellow flowers of prairie dock and compass plant to the pinks of the purple coneflower, Sullivant's milkweed, and blazing stars and the purples of the asters and Ohio spiderwort keep this area of perennial flowers exciting not only for the human eye but also for the birds and butterflies.

The Meadow Garden is also an excellent place to see a long display of color. Its best display is saved for fall when the ironweed and joe-pye weed are in their glory, but the false blue indigo and tall phlox make early summer almost as exciting. Each color is important because it attracts the particular visitor needed to carry on the species.

Fall is noted for its colorful leaves that add nutrients to the soil after they fall and are allowed to decay in place. They provide shelter for small animals, as do the hollow trees and stumps that add character to the yard. The nuts, or mast, from the trees give humans hints on what kind of year it has been and what kind of winter to expect and animals the food they need to survive. In turn, many plants depend on animals to bury their seeds so new plants can emerge in the spring. The shortening of the day signals all life to prepare for winter.

Nature is designed for long-term sustainability. The pawpaw tree, pitcher plant, and crossvine are wonderful examples of how nature has created each flower in such a way as to get its reproduction needs met. The brown blooms of the pawpaw attract its favorite pollinator, the fly. The pitcher plant's lovely hanging flowers have only one way in and another way out for insects that fly into its maze. The crossvine's trumpets are bicolored, in hopes that red will attract its favorite hummingbirds but,

Fern fronds

Southern pitcher plant

just in case they have not arrived this early in spring, that yellow will bring insects to visit its store of nectar and leave with pollen. Other plants work hard to keep certain insects away. The cup plant is designed to catch water in the cup that forms where the leaves meet the stem, thus preventing ants from reaching its yellow flowers before flying pollinators do.

The relationship between plants and animals helps sustain them both. Some pairings are highly specialized. The milkweed, for example, is the host plant for monarch butterflies, and the wild blue lupine is the only sustainer of the rare Karner butterfly. Without their special hosts, many birds and insects will not have their needs for sustainability met. Some birds, like the finches, find the seeds of the native prairie plants a fall feast that will help sustain them through the winter months. We have noticed that in the seven years we have been incorporating native plants into the Residence gardens, the variety of native wildlife has increased dramatically. The Heritage Garden is encouraging native flora and fauna to multiply. Native plants provide food and homes for a great variety of insects and larger animals that have coevolved into the biodiversity needed to sustain us all.

Ohio's geologic history laid the ground for plants to show us how they sustain themselves. The last 500 million years have given Ohio parts of five physiographic regions, each with a different bedrock, soil, and weather type and thus its own specialized plant communities (see appendix 1). These ecosystems meet in Ohio, which means that many plants are living on the edge of their preferred conditions. This gives the state a large number of threatened and endangered plants that need protection for their survival. Their sustainability is jeopardized by changing weather patterns, invasive nonnative plants, and human encroachment on the state's remaining wilderness. Most, if not all, of Ohio's endangered plant communities are threatened with extinction. Studying their adaptability to the home landscape and saving seeds are ways the Heritage Garden is helping native species survive.

The Heritage Garden has areas that mimic these diverse ecoregions and thus can help gardeners find native plants for

Spiderwort

Right:
Columbine,
Helen's Black
Rock

any type of conditions they face in their own yards. Some plants like the golden Alexander seem to do well in hot, dry, poor-soil prairie situations as well as in the cooler, darker areas of a shade garden. The inland sea oat is one of the few native ornamental grasses that thrives in light shade but tolerates sun very well. Blue pickerelweed loves to have wet feet so would adapt well to ponds. Silvery cinquefoil will become a groundcover under any condition. Ohio's native rhododendrons and mountain laurel do better in acid soils created from sandstone, while arborvitae likes more alkaline environments derived from limestone. The two outcrops in the Appalachian Garden make it easy to see which soil type plants prefer.

The most interesting story Ohio's plants tell is of their migration to survive our glacial history ten thousand years ago. As the land froze and was slowly covered by two-mile-high sheets of ice, seeds were carried southward by wind or animals and sprouted when they found an agreeable home. Some plants that are hardy enough to live in Ohio, and probably did at one time, migrated south and never made their way back. The Garden of the Lost holds several of these hardy southern plants such as the sweetbay magnolia and Alabama snow wreath.

As the glaciers retreated, boulders trapped in the ice left scars in the bedrock. Examples of this are seen in the striations on the alvar rocks and the groove in the glacial erratic, a sixteen-ton rock brought by ice from the Canadian Shield to Ohio that is now in the front yard. Plants soon realized that their favorite growing conditions were moving north too, and some began the slow process of following the cooler weather. The tamarack is one tree that worked its way south from Labrador to avoid the ice and then back. Some migrated northward only as far as the kettle lake bogs in Ohio, where they have stayed for the last ten thousand years. The Canadian hemlock is another example of northern boreal trees found in the Heritage Garden that are happy in some parts of our state. These trees illustrate the strong desire of plants to find places where they can thrive.

As the weight of the glaciers depressed the earth and allowed ocean waters to make their way to Ohio's shores, Atlantic coastal plants such as bearberry came on a one-way trip down the St. Lawrence Seaway. Some of these now live on the Headlands Sand Dune in the Residence's backyard.

Facing page:
Rhododendron

Glaciers were not the only cause of plant migrations. The bigleaf magnolia in the Pebbles Dolomite Outcrop came to Ohio with the Teays River, the ancient waterway

Compass plant
leaves

Magnolia leaves on moss

that flowed from the Carolinas into Indiana before the glaciers pushed it southward to form the Ohio River. This magnolia's only natural Ohio home is in Jackson County. This was the first of many plant-recorded examples of rivers or canals helping to transport the necessary genetic material for species reproduction.

After the glaciers melted, the state experienced a hot period that allowed a finger of the western prairies to advance across the state and bring ideal conditions for drought-resistant plants like gray-headed coneflower and prairie dock to become Ohio residents. As the weather cooled again, trees from the eastern forests began to expand their home on the west side of the Ohio River and created the vast beech and oak forests that sustained the Native Americans and frustrated the early pioneers.

Some plants in the Heritage Garden illustrate the deep genetic desire for the survival and sustainability of their species. The ginkgo, with its primitive fan-shaped leaf form, has its roots in the Permian period 225–280 million years ago. This tree was rescued from extinction by man's desire to have it growing in his garden and is a perfect example of how man can play a positive role in nature's sustainability.

There is so much to learn in the Heritage Garden about sustainability, not only about the way plants take care of themselves but also about their impact on man's efforts to survive. The cultural history of plants is fascinating and speaks to man's de-

sire to stay alive. The compass plant was used by the pioneers to tell directions. The flowering serviceberry told them when the ground was soft enough to dig. The hepatica is one of many examples in the garden of plants named after the body part whose ailment they were thought to cure. In this case, the shape of its leaves looks similar to the human liver and was thus given a name from the Greek for hepatitis by sixteenth-century observers who believed in the Doctrine of Signatures.

Ohio's first residents used many native plants as food, medicine, or dyes. The groundnut vine has a tuber that fed the hungry, the wild yam helped relieve cramps, and the bloodroot provided face paint for the Native Americans, who brought crops like corn, squash, and beans with them on their migrations. These stories in ethnobotany are fascinating illustrations of the ways that humans and plants have interacted for centuries in a mutually beneficial relationship. If we protect the biodiversity of nature, it will continue to provide the means to help us enjoy life.

Plants will survive in less than ideal situations, but they will thrive if they get their needs for water, sun, temperature, and soil type met and they will need a lot less effort from humans to do so. Using native plants in the right spots will lessen the demand on other natural resources and help sustain our universe. Less water, pesticides, fertilizers, and mechanical means of control mean a healthier planet for us all.

As more and more land is turned into suburbia, it is important to provide new avenues for animal and bird migrations, and that requires an unbroken path of their favorite foods and habitats. Backyards filled with water spots and native plants for food and shelter provide hope for sustaining our wildlife. Restoring and linking native ecosystems are becoming crucial in maintaining natural paths of migration and habitat. Every garden and yard can be part of this effort. Plants and animals do not abide by man's artificial boundaries.

By observing the shifting of plant and animal ranges, scientists are able to track the current period of global warming. It will be interesting to see which plants and animals move to better locales and thrive, which succumb to changing growing conditions, and which adapt to their new environments. Lessons for our own sustainability will be evident in the success of their efforts.

For some people, sustainability means a framework for avoiding catastrophe. One goal of the Ohio Governor's Residence and Heritage Garden is to help people realize that we must do better than the bare minimum if we hope to have a state that supports life to its fullest in the future. Plants are not optional. All the critical elements of life owe their foundation to plants. Plants clean the air and purify the water,

Azaleas and tulips near the front door

provide medicines, and feed humans and animals. Eighty-five percent of all the endangered species on earth are plants, yet we carelessly change our landscape without regard to the inhabitants those alterations destroy.

Homes supplied with power are not optional either. That is why solar panels have been installed and energy-efficient lightbulbs are used and compost is made and plastic products are biodegradable. That is why a green roof and bioswale are planned and use of native plants is promoted. That is why the sun's energy and rainwater are harvested in addition to fruits and vegetables. For it is by respecting nature and living in harmony with it that we have our best chance of surviving its long-term changes.

The Governor's Residence and Heritage Garden is a home and botanical garden where visitors can learn about native plants and the advantages of using them in their own gardens. It is an effort to encourage people to help sustain and preserve the fragile ecosystems that support our plant and animal life. It is a place where new ideas for saving energy both inside and outside the home can be seen in action. It is a place that can inspire sustainability of our planet and our livelihoods.

All the physical changes, the tours, the historic events, the seasons, and the progression of families truly make this property a "living museum" with a different exhibit on view each day. Each person who enters its gates adds something to its history and to its sustainability. Its evolving story continues to thrill its occupants and visitors.

The native plants in the Heritage Garden give the Governor's Residence a sense of place, reflect a regional identity, and convey how well we have served as stewards of our heritage. Like the objects within the Residence, indigenous plants tell the history of places, reflect who we are, and give clues to the strength of our commitment to our own future.

We invite you to join in our efforts to sustain a better future for all living things by using native plants in your landscape and maintaining an ecologically friendly home. Only by doing so will we be successful in our human struggle to endure.

We are planning for a hundred years by educating visitors today. Thanks to your help, the Friends of the Ohio Governor's Residence and Heritage Garden can do even more.

Ohio's Botanical Heritage

Guy Denny

THE state of Ohio occupies an area notable for its great geographic variety. Distinct physiographic regions harboring plants characteristic of western prairies, the Southwest, Canadian forests, the Atlantic coastal plain, and the Appalachian Mountains all converge in Ohio, creating an extremely rich and diversified landscape. In an effort to better familiarize Ohioans with the five major physiographic regions of Ohio and the plant species characteristic of each, garden plantings of native species replicating each of these physiographic regions have been established on the grounds of the Governor's Residence. A tour of the Ohio Heritage Garden allows visitors to see and learn firsthand about cranberry peat bogs, limestone barrens complete with glacial striations called alvars, Teays-age species, Lake Erie dunes, the Oak Openings, Bluegrass Section species, and much more. The Ohio Heritage Garden provides a unique educational opportunity for all Ohioans to experience the beauty and ecological diversity of the natural history of this great state of ours.

It has often been said that at the time of earliest settlement a squirrel could travel from limb to limb, tree to tree, all the way from the banks of the Ohio River

Wisteria

OHIO PHYSIOGRAPHIC PROVINCES & SECTIONS
by C. Scott Brockman

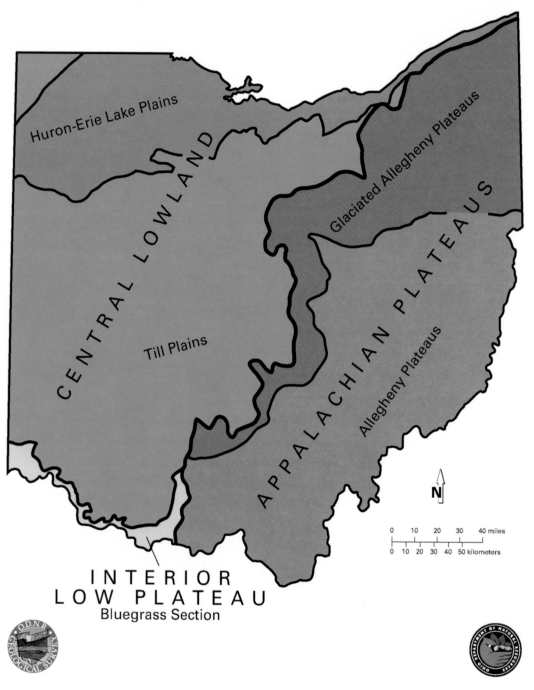

Huron-Erie Lake Plains

CENTRAL LOWLAND

Till Plains

Glaciated Allegheny Plateaus

APPALACHIAN PLATEAUS

Allegheny Plateaus

INTERIOR LOW PLATEAU

Bluegrass Section

N

| 0 | 10 | 20 | 30 | 40 miles |
| 0 | 10 | 20 | 30 | 40 | 50 kilometers |

Map of Ohio physiographic regions courtesy of the Ohio Geologic Survey

to the shores of Lake Erie without ever touching the ground. By all eyewitness accounts, the forest of early Ohio blanketed most of the landscape. Yet, within this matrix of vast forest, the landscape between the Ohio River and Lake Erie supported more than just forest cover. A closer look based on the detailed descriptions of the earliest land surveys reveals a rich and ecologically diverse landscape that included prairies, oak savannas, marshes, bogs and fens, swamps, oak openings, cedar barrens, deep gorges, and even alvars, all with their own characteristic plant assemblages. These plant communities were imbedded within the magnificent primeval forest, which in itself was also extremely diverse. This fascinating and ecologically rich diversity is a product of past geologic and climatic events responsible for molding the present landscape of Ohio. Scientists have broadly divided this part of the country into five major physiographic regions, each distinct geologically, topographically, and botanically: (1) Unglaciated Appalachian (Allegheny) Plateaus, (2) Central Lowland Till Plains, (3) Interior Low Plateau—Bluegrass Section, (4) Lake Plain, and (5) Glaciated Appalachian (Allegheny) Plateaus.

Unglaciated Appalachian (Allegheny) Plateaus

The oldest landscape in Ohio occupies the Unglaciated Appalachian (or Allegheny) Plateaus physiographic region of southeastern Ohio. This is an area of very rugged, heavily wooded, Appalachian hill country with the greatest landscape relief in the state. It is characterized by high hills and deep valleys cut into bedrock. Some hills are 1,200–1,400 feet above sea level. Much of the exposed bedrock is erosion-resistant Mississippian- and Pennsylvanian-Age sandstone, including the famous Blackhand Sandstone of the Hocking Hills region. Further east, the Pennsylvanian-Age bedrock comprises repetitive layers of sandstone, shale, coal, and clay with an occasional thin layer of limestone. Because of the ruggedness of the landscape and its infertile soils, this region is less populated and less developed than most of the rest of Ohio. Accordingly, there may be a greater diversity of plants and animals here than in any other region of the state. Some of the very rarest of these plants, such as bigleaf magnolia, fringetree, and umbrella magnolia, all of which are featured in the Heritage Garden, are disjuncts, normally found growing in the Appalachian Mountains far to the south of Ohio. They are believed to owe their presence in Ohio to the ancient, preglacial Teays River that had its headwaters in the Blue Ridge Mountains of the Carolinas and flowed northward across Virginia and West Virginia, entering Ohio just east of what is now Portsmouth and exiting westward near Celina. The Teays provided a corridor for the northerly range expansion of such species for around 200 million years before

Right:
Ohio coal

the beginning of the Ice Age, or Pleistocene. Other characteristic Appalachian species of plants like mountain laurel and pitch pine found within the Unglaciated Appalachian Plateau are typical of this type of unglaciated rugged terrain, while some plants found here are simply southern species growing at the extreme northern edge of their range, as is the case with crossvine and purple passionflower.

Although this region of Ohio has been heavily disturbed—first by the combined effects of strip-mining iron ore and limestone and of denuding the forests for fuel to feed the more than forty charcoal furnaces established here in the early 1800s, and later by deep and surface coal mining—the forests have made a remarkable comeback. Today, relatively young "second growth" forest covers more than 70 percent of the region, more than in any other part of Ohio. The forests in this part of the state are largely dominated by mixed oak woodlands and mixed mesophytic woodlands along with a limited number of yellow pine, pitch pine, and Virginia pine, which occupy the dry acid soils of ridgetops and south-facing slopes.

Central Lowland Till Plains

When the Appalachian Mountains were formed, the bedrock of Ohio was bowed upward into a low arch known as the Cincinnati Arch, running south to north. Over the next 200 million years, where this arch stood highest across the western half of the state the forces of erosion cut fastest and deepest all the way down to the soft layers of limestone bedrock. By the time the Ice Age began nearly 2 million years ago, what is now western Ohio had been eroded down to a relatively flat plain offering little resistance to the advancing glacial ice. Consequently, most of the landforms in the glaciated Till Plains are glacial deposits rather than bedrock as in the eastern half of our state, where the more erosion-resistant sandstone bedrock hills slowed and stopped the spread of glacial ice. Ohio was glaciated three and possibly four times during the Ice Age. Within the Till Plains, bedrock is typically covered by a thick blanket of glacially deposited soil known as till, which reshaped the Till Plains into a comparatively smooth rolling landscape. A significant exception occurs in Logan County, where an isolated massive bedrock hill known as the Bellefontaine Outlier survived the forces of erosion and rises 1,549 feet, the highest point in Ohio. The very fertile soils of the Till Plains provide some of our richest farmland. During

Facing page:
Magnolia trees
in the Governors'
Grove

pre-settlement times, these same soils supported our most extensive tallgrass prairie remnants, surrounded by forests dominated mostly by American beech and sugar maple trees. About four thousand to eight thousand years ago, during the postglacial Hypsithermal Interval, a period of warmer and drier weather than today's, prairies expanded eastward for a while, becoming part of the Ohio landscape. Today, approximately 95 percent of the Till Plains consists of farmland and urban development. South of the Bellefontaine Outlier, fast-flowing meltwaters from the glaciers filled valleys south of the ice front with enormous amounts of sand and gravel. Today, these buried valleys of porous outwash materials provide some of the most extensive groundwater sources in the state. In a few places within west-central Ohio, cold, alkaline groundwater emerges at the surface, creating fens or alkaline bogs such as Cedar Bog and Prairie Road Fen state nature preserves. Some of Ohio's rarest and most unusual plants, "living relicts of the Ice Age," such as shrubby cinquefoil, Canada burnet, Ohio goldenrod, and the white lady's-slipper orchid occur in these fens.

Interior Low Plateau—Bluegrass Section

The Interior Low Plateau—Bluegrass Section of Ohio, an extension of the vast Bluegrass Region of Kentucky, extends into most of Adams County, with smaller portions in the extreme southeastern parts of Brown and Highland counties. This small, roughly triangular area is characterized by ancient, reddish yellow, calcareous soils

and deep valleys carved out of easily eroded shale, often capped with more erosion-resistant limestone and dolomite rims that form massive steep cliffs and promontories such as those at the Buzzardroost Rock Preserve. These alkaline soils, at least those not touched by the Illinoian Glacier, are among the oldest in the state. The Bluegrass Section is also characterized by sinkholes, solution caves, rock crevices and overhangs, and juniper or eastern red cedar prairie openings.

Although many of the same prairie species found growing in the glaciated Central Lowland Till Plains, such as prairie dock, purple coneflower, and rattlesnake master, grow here as well, the prairies of the Bluegrass Section are believed to predate Wisconsinan glaciation. Two good examples of such prairies are Lynx Prairie and Chaparral Prairie nature preserves. Many of the rarest plant species found growing here, such as American aloe, rock sandwort, and Walter's violet, are more typical of the cedar glades in the Missouri Ozarks.

Other plants such as little gray polypody fern and Canby's mountain-lover, both extremely rare in Ohio and more characteristic of the Carolina Mountains, can also be found growing on the dolomite cliffs and boulders here. Within the narrow, cool, moist dolomite gorges, several northern or mountain species such as arborvitae or northern white cedar also occur. The oldest white cedars in Ohio, believed to be at least three hundred years old, grow in the Cedar Falls Preserve.

At the northern tip of the Bluegrass Section occurs the most fascinating geologic feature in Ohio, the Serpent Mound meteorite crater or cryptoexplosion structure. This is a five-mile-wide circular area where the bedrock is out of sequence, with

older rock on top of younger rock, as if the site had been struck long ago by a huge meteorite, which is the prevailing theory.

Because of its diverse landscape that supports relict plant communities of northern, southern, and western origin, the number of rare state-listed species of plants found growing in the Bluegrass Section is second only to the number occurring in the Oak Openings of northwestern Ohio.

Lake Plain

At the other end of the state, the Huron-Erie Lake Plain extends along the south shore of modern Lake Erie. During the Ice Age, meltwaters impounded between a wall of glacial ice to the north and the glacially deposited Fort Wayne End Moraine to the south formed a series of enormous glacial lakes with levels well above the present level of modern Lake Erie. At that time, lake waters covered much of what is now northwestern Ohio. Then, about 14,000 years ago, the Wisconsinan Glacier, the last of the continental glaciers to spread across Ohio, made its final retreat northward, freeing up the Niagara outlet. Lake levels dropped rapidly, exposing lake bottom across most of the northwestern corner of the state and eastward along a narrow strip paralleling but inland from the current Lake Erie shoreline. Drainage is extremely poor throughout this Lake Plain region due to the flatness of the landscape and the impervious clay soils that line the glacial lake basin.

When lake levels dropped, fine yellowish sands, washed into the glacial lake from what is now Michigan and deposited along the shoreline, were left high and dry to be redistributed across the land by wind. The most extensive of these deposits occurs in northwestern Ohio and covers an area of more than 150 square miles known as the Oak Openings. This is an area of sand barrens, prairies, sand dunes, wet sedge meadows, and woodlands of widely spaced stunted oaks, for which the region was named. Due to this variety of ecological communities, more state-listed species of plants such as wild lupine, spatulate-leaved sundew, and sweet-fern occur in the Oak Openings than in any other physiographic region of the state.

Left: Alvar

Right: Partridge pea in sand dune

Outside the Oak Openings but within the Lake Plain, where the exposed bed of the former glacial lake, based on a deep layer of muck, was flooded most of the year, an extensive swamp forest became established. Later this inhospitable area of about 1,500 square miles became known as the Great Black Swamp. Ohio's last wilderness, it was drained by the end of the 1800s and converted into some of Ohio's richest farmland.

Surrounding the shallow western basin of modern Lake Erie and Sandusky Bay, extensive marshes developed, along with their own characteristic plant communities and wetland wildlife. Other special features of the Lake Plain include the alvar communities of the Marblehead Peninsula and of Kelleys Island, with its famous glacial striations and grooves. One of Ohio's rarest plants, the Lakeside daisy, occurs in the alvar habitat on the Marblehead Peninsula and nowhere else in the United States. The well-developed beaches at the eastern end of Lake Erie are well known for their interesting Atlantic shoreline plants, including beach grass, inland sea rocket, and inland beach pea, which migrated westward shortly after the glaciers melted. The weight of the glacier had so compressed the bedrock that the Atlantic Ocean then extended into the present basin of Lake Ontario, forming a corridor for the westward migration of Atlantic coastal plants. Eventually, with crustal rebound of the compressed bedrock and the subsequent retreat of the ocean, these species became isolated from their Atlantic Coastal Plain origin.

Glaciated Appalachian (Allegheny) Plateau

Finally, just south of the extreme eastern portion of the Huron-Erie Lake Plain, we encounter the Glaciated Appalachian (or Allegheny) Plateau. Although continental glaciers easily flowed across the relatively level Till Plains of western Ohio, they were not able to advance very far into the Appalachian Plateau region, where high sandstone hills slowed and contained the southward and eastward movement of the ice. Where the glaciers were able to encroach on the plateau, especially in the northern half, the landscape is less hilly and the glacial soils more fertile, making the land more suitable for agriculture, and therefore for settlement. Reportedly, there are more people and industry within the Glaciated Appalachian Plateau than within any other physiographic region in the state. This region extends down and across the state from Ashtabula County in extreme northeastern Ohio south to the Paint Creek Valley and Highlands Nature Sanctuary south of Chillicothe, a distance of nearly 300 miles.

Northern Glaciated Appalachian Plateau

The very erodible soft shale bedrock in the more northerly portion of the plateau enabled the glaciers to override the landscape with relative ease, laying down glacial deposits as far south as northern Stark and Columbiana counties before encountering the solid, high sandstone hills of the Unglaciated Appalachian Plateau. Within the extreme northeastern portion of the Glaciated Appalachian Plateau, in an area known as the "Snow Belt," the characteristic forest cover of hemlock–white pine–northern hardwood forest is like that of the Allegheny forests of Pennsylvania and New York. A number of Allegheny Mountains plant species such as Carolina spring-beauty, painted trillium, and robin runaway occur nowhere else in Ohio. Also within the northern portion of the plateau, a deep, narrow, north-to-south canyon between two major lobes of the Wisconsinan Glacier, the Killbuck and Grand rivers, extended from Geauga County to Stark County. Torrents of glacial meltwaters coming from each lobe deposited an enormous amount of sand, gravel, clay, large cobbles, and even huge blocks of glacial ice in the canyon corridor between the two lobes. We find most of the best examples of sphagnum peat bogs and boreal fens in Ohio within this same corridor as a result of these huge buried blocks of ice later melting to form deep kettle bog lakes, and the large number of alkaline springs emerging from these extensive glacial deposits giving rise to alkaline fen communities.

Southern Glaciated Appalachian Plateau

The more southern leg of the Glaciated Appalachian Plateau follows the Appalachian Escarpment south along a narrow band where glacial ice moved eastward through valleys and over lower land for only a relatively short distance before being blocked by the higher sandstone hills of the Unglaciated Appalachian Plateau. In the western half of this southern section of the Glaciated Appalachian Plateau, extensive deposits of till and ground moraine from the Wisconsinan Glacier create a rolling landscape where American beech and sugar maple woodlands tend to dominate. However, the eastern half is typically covered with a relatively thin layer of more acidic glacial till from the older Illinoian glacier and has higher bedrock hills and deep gorges. Here, oak-hickory woodlands are more characteristic of the drier, more acidic, and much older shallow soils. Deep, narrow, cool, shaded, moist gorges within the Glaciated Appalachian Plateau, such as those associated with the Mohican, Chagrin, and Beaver Creek rivers, harbor Ice Age relict plants such as mountain maple, eastern hemlock, and red-berried elder and even nesting birds typical of more northern latitudes. At the extreme southern terminus of the Glaciated Appalachian Plateau within Paint Creek Valley, we encounter the deep dolomite gorge and cave complex of the Seven Caves Region, now the Highlands Nature Sanctuary. Here, too, a number of northern relict species, including Canada yew and northern white cedar, survive in the northern-like micro-climate of the deep gorges.

Native Plants of Ohio

Dewey Hollister

T HE plants described in this section are illustrated in the original botanical art by Dianne McElwain following page 81 in the text.

Native Plants of Ohio — The Prairie Heritage Garden

Prairie dock (*Silphium terebinthinaceum*), rough blazing star (*Liatris aspera*), Sullivant's milkweed (*Asclepias sullivantii*), royal catchfly (*Silene regia*), and purple coneflower (*Echinacea purpurea*) represent the Prairie Garden.

Prairie dock's cluster of huge upturned leaves led some to call it elephant ear. From midsummer until September, its small sunflower-like blooms hover high above the ground on leafless stems. It is joined in bloom by rough blazing star. When in full glory, this plant resembles purple exclamation marks in the landscape.

New England aster and goldenrod

Sullivant's milkweed is also called prairie milkweed, since its presence indicates healthy prairie. This early- to midsummer bloomer was discovered in Ohio.

Royal catchfly's red orange blooms are tailor-made for hummingbirds and attract them to the Prairie Garden. It grows tall and slender to keep its flowers clear of surrounding plants. Royal catchfly and purple coneflower share an early- to later-summer bloom period. Purple coneflower, unlike almost any other prairie plant, has been bred into an amazing array of garden forms; however, the wild form with its downward-swept petals is hard to improve upon. As shown in the painting, purple coneflower is very attractive to butterflies such as the monarch butterfly (*Danaus plexippus*). In fact, the monarch butterfly could live its entire life cycle with this collection of plants, since monarch caterpillars feed only on milkweeds.

Native Plants of Ohio—The Meadow Heritage Garden

False sunflower (*Heliopsis helianthoides*), tall ironweed (*Vernonia gigantea*), pokeweed (*Phytolacca americana*), mistflower (*Conoclinium coelestinum*), and hedge bindweed (*Calystegia sepium*) represent the Meadow Garden.

False sunflower is in many ways a better garden plant than true sunflowers. It can stand some shade, blooms nearly the entire summer, and comes back from a tough root system every year.

Tall ironweed lives up to its name in not only being tall but also being tough as iron. Its late-summer flowers are the ultimate in dark purple coloring of any native plant.

A large pokeweed can resemble a small, maroon-stemmed tree. In fact, with the stem leaves removed, the effect can be striking. The graceful arching flower racemes are soon set with attractive green berries. These turn purple at maturity but should be removed before this on cultivated specimens to reduce weight.

Mistflower is also called wild ageratum due to its resemblance to that exquisite blue-flowered annual. Like tall ironweed, mistflower is a butterfly magnet and is shown here with a clouded sulphur butterfly (*Colias philodice*); its short spreading habit makes this native plant an excellent, late summer–blooming ground cover.

Hedge bindweed's aggressive vining native nature can indeed bind all manner of plants to one another. But its pinkish white morning-glory flowers are beautiful, and the plant does not need to be planted each year like annual morning glories.

Magnolia macrophylla—Bigleaf Magnolia

At first glance, a bigleaf magnolia is reminiscent of a tropical tree. As the name implies, the leaves are gigantic, and the tree has flowers to match (salad-bowl size). In fact, bigleaf magnolia has the largest leaves and flowers of any tree native to North America with the exception of some native palms, which have larger leaves. This species is one of three magnolias native to Ohio and by far the rarest, and is found only in Jackson County. It is usually regarded as a Teays River plant. The Teays River was the predecessor of the Ohio River and flowed from North Carolina into southern Ohio east of Portsmouth. From there it flowed into Central Ohio and then westward to the Mississippi River. Many Appalachian plants followed this corridor into South-eastern Ohio. Nearly everywhere the tree is found, it is an understory tree; the large leaves catch what light makes it down through the taller trees. The Appalachian Garden contains specimens from seedling to blooming size. On breezy days, the silvery undersides of the great leaves can be seen from a long way off.

Nelumbo lutea—American Lotus

The name lotus conjures up images of exotic Asian locations and the tropics, but there is a lotus native to North America as well. The Asian or sacred lotus is by far

the better known of the two, with a natural range that extends far beyond the Asian tropics and occurs from Russia to Australia. North America's lotus or water chinquapin is every bit as grand a plant as the Old World lotus. It differs mainly in having creamy yellow flowers as opposed to pink. All lotus have water-repellant leaves that bead water drops into silvery balls. The plants overwinter in cold climates by dying down to edible tubers. In spring the first leaves emerge and rest on the surface of the water like a water lily. If the water is deep, all later leaves will float as well, but in shallow areas they rise up umbrella fashion. Aggressive runners then spread out in the mud, forming new leaves and, before winter, new tubers. This is why the lotus in the Water Garden have pools to themselves. The spectacular flowers give rise to pepper shaker/honeycombed seedpods, often seen in dried arrangements. The painting depicts the entire growing season. American lotus occurs naturally in scattered locations across Ohio. Once established, it can form truly large colonies.

Bignonia capreolata—Crossvine

The lower left corner of the painting illustrates the origin of the name crossvine. When a stem is cut, a cross shape is seen inside. Another theory is that the name is derived from the cross shape of the new climbing growth. The leaves are actually trifoliate (three leaflets), but the center leaf has been modified into a branching tendril for climbing. Crossvine is in the same family as the trumpet creeper and the catalpa tree, but its closest relatives live in the American tropics. Not surprisingly, crossvine is most abundant in the south. The Ohio plants are nearly all within one mile of the Ohio River and represent some of the northernmost individuals of the species. The Wall Garden contains plants from Hamilton, Clermont, Brown, and Adams counties. This is a great plant for masonry walls, since the tendrils will cling to the surfaces and the evergreen leaves flush purple for winter interest. In May, the gorgeous orange-red tube flowers with yellow lips bloom for nearly a month. Isolated individuals often do not bear the long flattened pods, so cross-pollination seems to be needed. The plants in the Wall Garden have born abundant pods and fertile seed every year.

Sarracenia purpurea—Pitcher Plant and
Vaccinium macrocarpon——Cranberry

Cranberries

Pitcher plants are carnivorous. Their pitcher-shaped leaves are both traps and stomachs. Nectar glands around the entrance attract insects to visit and entice them down into the mouth. Here slick areas cause the insect to slip, and down-pointing hairs prevent its escape. The fluid-filled bottom soon drowns the prey. Bacteria and digestive enzymes release nutrients for the plant to absorb. Unlike animals, however, pitcher plants make their food from the sun. The insects provide missing nutrients that their cold, acidic bog habitat cannot. In northern Ohio these bogs were formed by melting glacial ice blocks. Sphagnum mosses control these remnant bogs by evaporating large amounts of water, thus refrigerating the habitat. These cold, acid conditions do not allow much decomposition to fertilize plants. Cranberries thrive in these conditions. Their common name is a corruption of crane berry. The small white flowers remind some of a crane's head.

Both pitcher plants and cranberries can be found in the Kettle Lake Bog.

Passiflora incarnata 'Ammon's Blue'

Of all Ohio's native plants, none look more exotic or tropical than our passionflower (*Passiflora incarnata*), which is the hardiest of its kind in the world. Flower size can range from two inches in diameter to four inches, as in the case of 'Ammon's blue', which is larger in all its parts than the species. The passionflower vine climbs with tendrils to an ultimate annual height of twenty feet or more. Flowers begin to appear in July and continue until October or even November if grown on a sunny, protected wall (as is the case at the Heritage Garden). Each flower opens in the early afternoon and wilts the next morning, but new buds open each day. In sunny, warm conditions most flowers are followed by a fruit that is largely air-filled, the seeds in the middle being in individual sacs of delicious passionfruit juice. Usually the peduncle (flower stalk) lengthens as the fruit forms, allowing it to dangle below the foliage. 'Ammon's blue' is unusual in that the peduncle lengthens while in bud, so the flowers dangle and are oriented face-on to an observer. Carpenter bees are frequent pollinators, and ants are recruited by the vine for protection. The ants patrol the passionflower, chasing off potential vine-eating insects and being fed nectar in return. Like many of its tropical cousins, *Passiflora incarnata* has nectar glands near each leaf and under each flower. The fragrance of the flower is reminiscent of sweet musky lemons. 'Ammon's blue' was found in Clermont County, Ohio. It is named for Ammon Hollister, who undoubtedly planted the seed that became 'Ammon's blue' by eating passionfruit from other vines and spitting out the seeds.

Passionflowers can be found on the Wall Garden.

Trillium and
foam flowers

Trillium grandiflorum—
Large-Flowered Trillium

The large-flowered trillium is Ohio's state wild-flower with good reason. Besides occurring throughout the state, it is the showiest spring wildflower. In rich woods it can form massive carpets of color. The flowers open snowy white and fade to a beautiful pink. Trillium is derived from the Latin word for three: all parts of the plant are in threes. Always rare in northwestern Ohio, it has become rare in many other regions due to habitat disturbance/destruction. Like many woodland wildflowers, trillium is slow to reestablish itself and grows slowly. Today, Appalachian Ohio has some of the best remaining populations. Trillium seeds are spread by ants. Each seed has an elaiosome, a fleshy outgrowth that is eaten by ants in the nest. The seed is deposited in the debris pile, and the ant waste is ideal for the young seeds, keeping them moist. It is most appropriate that the large-flowered trillium is the symbol for the Heritage Garden. It started from humble beginnings and continues to grow more beautiful with each passing year.

The large-flowered trillium is a highlight of the Woodland Wildflower Garden in the spring.

*Aesculus glabra—*Ohio Buckeye

The Ohio buckeye represents Ohio well as its state tree since it occurs in the majority of counties. However, the areas where the tree is absent are almost all nonglaciated regions. The yellow buckeye, Ohio's only other native buckeye, is nearly restricted to those very areas. Hybrids are thus rarely found. Both of Ohio's buckeyes are unknown on the East Coast and so were among the trees found only after explorers arrived west of the Appalachian Mountains. The buckeye's seeds reminded the explorers of a deer's or buck's eye. The Native Americans knew the tree well and used the seeds as food. This is no easy task, since the raw seeds are toxic enough in some species to

be used as a fish poison. However, when properly washed and prepared, the seeds yield a good flour. Buckeyes often grow under taller trees in the forest and their bronzy-colored new leaves are the first tree leaves to be seen in early spring. Ohio buckeye, unfortunately, also loses its leaves equally early in the fall or even late summer. Yellow buckeye leaves are more durable. It has become a tradition for people, especially in Ohio, to carry buckeye seeds with them for luck.

Buckeye trees grow in the eastern and western edges of the Heritage Garden.

Buckeye flowers

*Erythronium americanum—*Yellow Trout Lily

The yellow trout lily is one of Ohio's most beautiful spring ephemerals: a plant that races through its growing cycle as soon as temperatures allow. It dies down to a dormant state before other taller plants can shade it out. Generally, these are woodland plants living on the forest floor, and sunlight is available only until the trees grow their leaves. Yellow trout lily is usually found in rich woods throughout the state. The name "trout lily" comes from the plant's mottled leaves, which suggest the skin of a brook trout. Other common names for this plant are "fawn lily," since the dappled pattern resembles a young deer, and "dogtooth violet," derived from the white bulb-like corms that resemble a dog's tooth. While there are native yellow violets, there is virtually no resemblance to an *Erythronium* of any kind. Yellow trout lily often grows in large colonies.

Yellow trout lilies grow in the Woodland Wildflower Garden.

Sanguinaria canadensis—Bloodroot

The vivid white flowers of bloodroot are just about the first sign of spring in Ohio's richer forests. The plants look like they are wearing coats, since a large leaf is wrapped around every flower stem. While the flower is short-lived, the leaves last well into the summer. The painting shows bloodroot through its entire growing season and the origin of the name. When a root is cut, a blood red sap oozes out. This was used by Native Americans as body paint and as topical medicine because of the alkaloid sanguinarine. Sanguinarine is an antibacterial, antifungal, and anti-inflammatory chemical. However, the FDA considers bloodroot unsafe even in tiny amounts. So the poppy relative should be admired for its beauty and left in its woodland home.

Bloodroot can be found in the Woodland Wildflower Garden.

Contributors

Ian Adams is an environmental photographer, writer, and teacher based in Cuyahoga Falls, Ohio. More than 4,500 of his color landscape and garden photographs have been published, and he has conducted over 130 seminars and workshops in nature, digital, and garden photography. Fifteen books of his photography have been published, including *The Art of Garden Photography* (Timber Press).

Guy Denny retired as chief of the Division of Natural Areas and Preserves of the Ohio Department of Natural Resources after thirty-three years of public service. He is the former executive director of the Ohio Biological Survey. A graduate of the University of Toledo, Guy has published widely on Ohio's natural history.

Dewey Hollister has been a landscape designer and garden lecturer in Cincinnati, Ohio, for more than twenty years. He has worked on projects from Ohio to the Bahamas and from Africa to China. Dewey has been actively involved in the Heritage Garden from its first day to the present.

Mary Alice Mairose received a BA from Northern Kentucky University and an MA in American History from the Ohio State University. As curator at the Governor's Residence, she has conducted extensive research on the property and its occupants, and has developed the Residence docent program.

Botanical artist Dianne McElwain works from her home-studio in Cincinnati, Ohio. Dianne is a member of the American Society of Botanical Artists in New York City. Her botanical art has won numerous awards, and her paintings are found in prestigious collections throughout the United States and in London, England.

Gary W. Meisner, FASLA, received his BSLA from Michigan State University. He is partner at Meisner and Associates/Land Vision Landscape Architects & Planners in Cincinnati and has created designs and master plans for public spaces in Ohio and surrounding states since 1970. Elected Fellow of the American Society of Landscape

Water Garden

Architects by his peers in 1989, Gary has received more than fifty other awards and commendations.

Foam flower and
May apple

BARBARA POWERS heads the Inventory and Registration Department of the Ohio Historic Preservation Office, part of the Ohio Historical Society. A graduate of Miami University with a BA in American Studies, she received a Master of Architectural History and a Certificate in Historic Preservation from the University of Virginia. Barbara has researched and lectured on late-nineteenth- and early-twentieth-century Ohio architecture.

FRANCES STRICKLAND moved from Kentucky to Ohio when she married Ted Strickland in December 1987. She received a doctorate in educational psychology from the University of Kentucky and spent most of her professional life working in the public school system. As first lady, she is chair of the Family and Children First Council and supports her husband's education, energy, and health care initiatives.

TED STRICKLAND grew up in Scioto County as the eighth of nine children. His resume includes serving in the ministry and as a children's home director, psychologist, and college professor before his election to the U.S. House of Representatives in 1992. He represented Ohio's 6th Congressional District for twelve years and then in 2006 was elected governor.

HOPE TAFT, First Lady of Ohio 1999–2007, moved to Ohio in 1972 when her husband, Bob Taft, entered the University of Cincinnati Law School. As first lady, she realized the need of Ohioans to connect with the Governor's Residence and instituted many programs to make their visit a meaningful experience. The development of the curator's position, the introduction of a trained docent program for volunteer guides, the creation of the Friends of the Ohio Governor's Residence and Heritage Garden, and the installation of the Heritage Garden were four of these initiatives that combined her love of history and gardening with the educational mission of the Residence.

Shooting star